MW01708694

Elizabeth,

Happy Graduation !!

[signature]

DO THE RIGHT THING

MAKE ETHICS YOUR BRAND

BY JEFFREY G. COLLINS

Do the Right Thing: Make Ethics Your Brand

ISBN: 978-0-9908600-0-6
ISBN: 978-0-9908600-1-3

For more information, to order books, or
to book Jeff as a speaker, contact:
Attorney Jeffrey G. Collins jcollins@collinslegal.net
Book is available on Amazon.com

Table of Contents

Dedication

This book is dedicated to my children, Justin and Jessica.

Acknowledgments

This book would not have been possible without the support of many people. First, thanks to my wife, Lois, who has lived and breathed the entire project. I appreciate her encouragement throughout this adventure. Special thanks to Eric Miller for planting the visionary seed for me to write the book.

Many thanks to Diane Reeder, for her steadfast support and guidance. Thanks to Sharon Banks of Bankable Marketing Strategies, LLC for getting us to the finish line. I could not have walked through the literary forest without them.

Thanks to Victoria Seabrooks and Leila Miller for their excellent line editing. Thanks to Danielle Funderburg of funDESIGN and Galen T. Pauling of Mad Traffic Creative Services, LLC for the cover design and book layout. Thanks to Imad Hamad for his candid and insightful interview. Finally, thanks to my parents, Dr. and Mrs. James Collins, for being my ethical role models and exposing me to a variety of life experiences that provided the perspective for the book.

There are few life defining moments more daunting than when your jury says, "We have reached a verdict." Who is your jury?

Introduction

Only a few months earlier, the client was sitting behind a mahogany desk with a matching credenza conducting a high-powered conference call. Now, he was sitting at a large wooden rectangle table in a federal courtroom awaiting a verdict.

It didn't seem possible. Only a few months earlier, he was on top of the world. Now, he feared the world was on top of him. He had given legal advice to an upstart health care business, and found himself the subject of a federal indictment.

Did his advice cross the line? Was his instruction on billing illegal? Would all of the years of schooling be wasted? Would all the years spent building his career be pointless? What would happen to his family if the jury were to say "guilty?" How would they survive?

And, even if he survived this, what would be his brand?

The jury now enters the courtroom. The extra security signals finality to a three-year ordeal. Federal marshals strategically position themselves. Some are stationed at the exit door and others stand in the aisle of the courtroom. One marshal sits right behind the defendant. This show of force catches the eye of everyone in the courtroom. Throughout the two-week trial there had only been one marshal in the courtroom. There were no outbursts or threats of violence during the trial. Was the judge sending a message? Was this standard practice?

Before the verdict is announced, the client pulls out a picture from his wallet of his wife and three sons. He stares at the picture. Moments before he faces judgment, he clings to the picture that is now cupped in the palm of his hand. At that second, he would trade all of the trappings of success to remain with family. He wonders what went wrong. He wonders how he ever got in this position where he now has no control over his fate.

I was at a little league game with my son, enjoying the bright day and remembering when my father did the same thing with me. It was a great game, and his team won, but that wasn't the point for me. The point for me is that my child was playing in the sunshine, learning about integrity and practice and teamwork… and having fun!

Imagine my dismay when I heard one of the parents. He sauntered up to the sandlot after the game ended. He didn't ask: "Did you have fun?" He didn't ask: "What did you learn?" Or "Did you make any friends?" Or "Were you a good teammate?" Or even "Were you satisfied with how you played?" Instead, he asked one question that let me know exactly what kind of person he was. He asked:

"Did you win the game?"

Sadly, his emphasis was entirely on the finish line. Nothing mattered except the checkmark in the "win/loss" column.

What happens as a result of that fateful question? The son ends up caring only about the outcome. After all, that's all his parent cared about. The value of sportsmanship is tragically lost. The value of playing hard is lost. The value of training was lost. The value of having the courage to compete was lost. The struggle and sacrifice that leads to victory or defeat was lost. This dad was only interested in "winning"—as he described it.

Danger comes when you attach self-worth to winning or losing. You are not a better person because you won, nor are you a worse person because you lost. Victory comes from giving it your honest, best effort. Your ethical compass gets misdirected if the emphasis is solely on the result instead of the process. When the focus is solely on the bottom line and not the journey to arrive at the finish line, we are at risk of creating leaders with no ethics. It matters how you accomplish the end.

When you put character first, you define success differently: not by how much money you made or how high you went up the ladder or how many games you won, but by your reputation, and by how closely you followed your ethical compass. The way you traveled through difficult terrain says volumes about your character. Ethics becomes your brand. A good name becomes your personal calling card.

As an attorney, a prosecutor, and a judge, I have been in countless positions where I had to make difficult ethical decisions. I have had to balance the demands of justice against defending unsympathetic clients. I have had to balance public safety against treading on individual rights. I have taken positions that were unpopular in my community and with some of the people closest to me. This book is about my personal journey developing my ethical "brand."

It is all about the journey.

Developing character starts at a young age. Fast forward twenty-five years, and see this same little league player thrust into an ethically challenging situation. He may be an attorney who is obsessed with winning and not apt to play by the rules. Or, a corporate executive obsessed with making money, succumbing to a temptation to cook the books. Or, a physician blinded by greed, billing for services that are not rendered.

We have a serious breakdown in principled leadership. The challenges start at a young age.

When the focus is exclusively on the result, students may cheat on a test, job hunters may pad a resume and politicians may accept a kickback. Ethical potholes are more likely to be created when there is a repeated directive to get the job done and attention is not paid to how you get the job done.

Years ago, I attended the funeral of Justice James Brickley of the Michigan Supreme Court. I never met Justice Brickley. His son spoke at the funeral. The son said his father told the family long ago that when he died he would not leave the family a lot of money. Dedicating his life to public service did not make Justice Brickley a financially rich man. However, his son said his dad "promised to leave me something greater: a good name."

A good name is priceless. A good name is worth a fortune. Not having the word "scandal" and "Brickley" in the same sentence is a good thing.

Leaving as your legacy "a good name" is what this book is all about. It doesn't take much: just your wholehearted commitment to courage, character and compassion, the three pillars for a good name and strong ethical leadership. It takes courage to accept the responsibility of leadership. It takes character to do the right thing time and time again when an ethical challenge arises. It takes true compassion to want to leave whatever you touch, whether it is a job, a university, a community or a relationship, better than you found it. Whenever you begin your journey, wherever you are in your journey, you can strive for integrity. You can be "that guy" who is known to do the right thing time and time again. I encourage everyone to make ethics their brand.

One of the great joys of my life has been watching my children grow up playing baseball, softball, basketball and tennis. Principles learned on the field can translate into success years later. These lessons form the foundation for strong ethical leaders. I have therefore organized the chapters into sports metaphors, to show how those lessons translate into real- life challenges and solid life principles. Don't let a criminal trial be your "wakeup call" to realize what is important in life. When the jury announces your verdict, you do not want to be found guilty of an ethical transgression which sacrifices your good name. This book celebrates the birth and growth of sound ethical leadership. The journey starts here.

CHAPTER ONE

Spring Training

Every professional baseball season starts with spring training. Spring training gives players a chance to practice and play exhibition games before the start of the regular season. Players use spring training to get physically and mentally prepared for the long grind of the regular season. A productive spring training can set the team up for a productive regular season. Spring training also gives coaches the opportunity to assess the strengths and weaknesses of the team. The scouting report about you is the beginning of your "brand."

Think of the time spent getting ready to face life's ethical challenges as an ethical "spring training." Just as a good spring training sets the team up for the season, lessons learned growing up provide foundational "spring training" for ethical leadership. We all have ethical role models. There is someone we can all point to whether it is a parent, a relative, a sibling, a teacher, a coach, a neighbor or a friend that helped to shape and mold our ethical character.

I did not have to look far for an ethical role model. I distinctly remember being six years old and in a grocery store with my mother. We were in the checkout line and I picked up a candy bar and surreptitiously put it in my pocket. In the parking lot my mom noticed the candy bar I had prepared to eat. She said, "How did you get that candy bar?" I proudly claimed, "I took it." Despite my successful completion of the crime, my mom pointed out to me that we did not pay for it. She said emphatically, "The candy bar is not yours." She asked me, "How would you feel if you owned the store?" Instead of looking the other way or waiting until later to correct my ethical misdeed, my mom marched me and the half-eaten candy bar right back into the store. She paid for it, made me apologize to the cashier and made me throw away the uneaten half. My mom also said "When your dad gets home, he is going to give you a good talking to." I learned valuable ethical lessons from the candy bar experience:

Recognizing that there is a victim is a key component of ethical leadership.

Often people rationalize unethical behavior by saying, "What's the problem? Nobody got hurt." This is particularly true when the victim is the public at large. If I am robbed at gunpoint, there is a clear victim. However, the victim is more abstract when the public at large is cheated. No matter how distant the harm may appear to be, ethical leaders are able to identify a victim.

The ethical leader not only identifies a victim, but he also has empathy toward the victim. The ethical leader is sensitive to the suffering the victim will endure. He is able to put himself in the shoes of the victim. The thought of a victim facing any harm becomes a deterrent to unethical behavior. Talking to my dad following the candy bar heist, I felt like a defendant appearing before the court for sentencing. Having to explain to Dad and reflect on what I did triggered another ethical deterrent: shame. The deterrent that keeps many people from committing unethical acts is public embarrassment. How would you like it if your misdeeds were on the front page of the newspaper or the lead story on the evening news? The shame you would feel if the unethical act is discovered by people you respect should propel you to do the right thing. You should always endeavor to protect your reputation and shield your brand.

In my ethical spring training, I also learned the value of positive reinforcement. My mom always had a word of encouragement. She consciously searches for the compliment. She always has a kind word. She believes unless you have something good to say about someone, you should not say anything at all. Looking to identify and highlight the talents of others has proven to be a good lesson in ethical leadership. Ethical leaders recognize there is a basic human desire to be affirmed and validated. Ethical leaders constantly acknowledge this desire and are not shy about recognizing it. Ethical leaders are humble enough to broadcast the praise.

During my ethical spring training, I also learned the value of persistence and toughness. To change a culture requires toughness. There will be push back. There will be times you will have to make tough decisions. There will be times you will have to stand alone. There will be times you have to make unpopular decisions. I draw strength from my ethical role models in giving me the strength to stand tall in the midst of the storm of peer disapproval.

My dad has the strongest handshake I have ever felt. It is an unyielding grip that will potentially fracture your hand if you are caught unaware. At my swearing-in ceremony for Detroit Recorder's Court, the zipper on my judicial robe got stuck. The audience patiently paused before applauding. My wife tried to pull it up, but the zipper was unrelenting. It was not moving. The audience continued to wait. I could not zip it. My mom could not zip it. Out of nowhere, my dad with one swift movement grabbed the robe with his left hand and zipped it with no problem with the rigid command of his right hand.

My dad's handshake gives you insight into how he takes charge of situations. He is someone you can count on. When he makes a promise, he will keep it. He is someone who is never late. He is the only person I know who has gone through life without an alarm clock.

Growing up, my dad used to tell me and my brother, "When you meet someone, always look them in the eye and give them a firm handshake." There is an ethical branding lesson in my dad's counsel—and in his example. Your word is your bond. When you make a promise you keep it. When you make a commitment you honor it. Honesty is the core of ethical leadership. To look someone in the eye connotes strength. The determined handshake symbolizes commitment and reliability.

At the time my dad was handed a diploma from Detroit Northern High School in 1944, he was told he would never be a doctor. Obviously they did not know the strength of the hand they were shaking. Unbeknownst to his cynics, my dad went on to graduate from Wayne State University and then go on to be one of two African Americans in his graduation class at the University of Michigan Medical School. His pediatric practice has spanned more than fifty years, and he has provided medical care in many instances to three generations.

I drew inspiration from my dad's journey as I struggled to get into law school. To go to law school, you have to take a standardized test called the LSAT. Standardized test-taking has never been my strength. I did so poorly on the test that I got rejected from Northwestern University School of Law in ten days. I had heard of early admissions, but never early rejections! More than 95% of the people taking the test scored better than me. My counselor said, "It looks like the only question you got right was your name." I thanked him for the pep talk and explained that anyone can have a bad day. I took the test again, and did even worse proving that I was having more than one bad day. Despite the low scores, I still applied to many law schools. I refused to let surrender be my brand.

I was flatly rejected from every law school in Illinois. Not to be deterred, I decided that I would direct my efforts to my home state of Michigan. Once again, I got shut out. I was rejected by fifteen law schools. It is ironic that the law school where I would teach for years and receive the highest possible faculty evaluations—Wayne State University— rejected me as a student. All of my earnings from summer jobs went to law school applications and I had nothing to show for it. It got to the point I could identify a rejection by the size of the envelope. All of my friends were getting big envelopes with housing and registration papers stuffed inside. All of my envelopes were real small. All you need room for was one sheet of paper to give the "no, you can't come here" response.

I decided to apply to Howard University School of Law in Washington, D.C. I could tell from the application process that Howard was different from the rest. It was the only school that asked for letters of recommendation. It was the only school that required an autobiographical statement explaining why you wanted to go to law school. After a few months of waiting, a big envelope finally came to the door. It was from Howard University School of Law. Like my dad, I learned determination. Staying the course through persistence is a valuable ethical lesson.

Good things can happen if you stay the course. It is tempting and sometimes easy to wave the white flag, to throw in the towel and quit. You can think a situation is hopeless… and out of nowhere a breakthrough happens! It occurs if you keep pushing the envelope and refuse to surrender.

My Spring Training: Tennis!

I was fortunate that my dad introduced me to a sport that helped to define my ethical code. Tennis became a major part of my life. I played junior tournaments, high school tennis and ultimately tennis for Northwestern University. What makes amateur tennis unique is the code of conduct. There are no umpires. There are no referees. Players are left to call the lines themselves. Players have to police their own conduct. There could come a key time in the match when your opponent hits a ball that lands right on the line. If you call it "out" you will win the point and possibly the match. The call you make is final. There is no appeal. If you call the ball "in" you will lose the point and possibly the match. For the novice, this could present an ethical dilemma.

There is nothing worse in tennis than having a reputation as a "hooker." That's when, as a player, you make an incorrect call to get ahead of your opponent. You call an "in" ball "out," for example, to avoid losing the point. A tennis player gets "hooked" when his or her opponent intentionally makes a bad call. Of course, the player with character will make the right call. He takes no pride in winning by cheating. The principled player does not want the win tainted by a bad call, and most importantly does not want to develop a reputation as a "hooker." An ethical tennis player, like an ethical lawyer, would rather lose a match or a case honestly than to win by cheating. The main check and balance on the tennis player is the player's own conscience.

Making the right call time and time again builds ethical character and it builds your brand. Playing competitive tournament tennis taught me to take pride in making trustworthy judgments. I learned early to take pride in doing the right thing.

The junior tennis circuit also teaches you how to deal with being the recipient of a bad call. When that happens, do you yell and scream? Do you lose your temper? Do you hit your opponent with the racquet? Often, your opponent deliberately makes a "bad" call in hopes that you will lose control, not only immediately following the call, but for the rest of the game as well. They continue to make errant calls in order to have an enduring, distracting effect beyond the one contested point.

But crying over spilled milk does not allow you to replay the point. Finding the strength to disagree while ignoring the distraction is a part of character development, and what I learned during my college tennis matches.

Keeping your focus in the midst of an unfair call is a valuable lesson. Ethical leaders must take the high road. In politics it is called a "thick skin." The unfair attacks and cheap shots are even more common in politics than they are in tennis. But the ethical leader does not take the bait. Ethical leaders remain above the fray. Ethical leaders resist the temptation to hurl insults back. Some tennis players after receiving a bad line call will return the favor on the next point and intentionally make a bad call to even the score. Ethical leaders must resist the temptation to exact revenge.

Revenge (n): an inappropriate reaction to a perceived harm to get even.

Staying "above the fray" means that you always act with civility. Vigorous debate—in sports and in life—is healthy. However, people should be able to disagree without flying off the handle. The tone of your conversations, especially in a professional setting, must remain civil and respectful. The debate should never get personal. Name-calling is out of bounds. The debate should never deteriorate to the point where adults act more like children. Ethical leaders, no matter how heated the debate becomes, must remain the adult in the room and always safeguard their brand.

After every tennis match you shake hands. Even if you despise your opponent, as a matter of custom you shake hands. Not shaking hands is poor, poor sportsmanship. Lessons learned on the tennis court in civility, fair play, staying above the fray, and remaining the adult have helped to strengthen my ethical core.

Blame-Shifting is NOT Ethical Conduct

I have been at far too many junior baseball, softball and basketball games where the umpire gets blamed for the result. I am amazed at some of the insults umpires receive. The umpire, who quite frankly does not have a dog in the fight, shows tremendous restraint in ignoring the insults. One day, I would love to hear a parent yell from the stands at a referee who missed a foul their kid made. Where is the balance? All of the vitriol is one-sided. I have seen umpires at a girls' softball game need a protective escort to the parking lot to prevent collisions with angry parents.

What message is being sent when parents dump on the umpire? Clearly, it shows no respect for authority. Also, it sends the message, "If you lose, it is because of the umpires." I have seen parents extend the criticism to the coach and even the teammates of their child. Blaming third parties provides the youngster with a built-in excuse. It deflects attention away from the play of the child. Blame-shifting does not help to build a strong ethical base of personal responsibility.

Ethical Leaders Are Accountable

The junior tennis circuit was also unique in that there was a "no coaching" rule. Strategy and shot selection are all left for the player to figure out. There are no halftime speeches. There are no time outs. The "no coaching" rule teaches you to take ownership of the outcome. If things go wrong, you have no one else to blame. You cannot blame the coach, nor can you blame a teammate. This promotes an important feature of ethical leadership, namely accountability.

Too often people do not take ownership of their mistakes. Once I had a client who came to me after he was convicted by a jury. His next court appearance was the sentencing. I stressed how important it was for him to say he was sorry and to admit his mistakes. It took months of meetings and at least ten draft statements before he could admit the wrong he committed. The stubbornness was due to his inability to take ownership of his wrong conduct. Once the client was able to write, in his own words, a **full, excuse-free admission of guilt**, then and only then could we see an ethical breakthrough.

An alcoholic cannot be helped until he admits he is an alcoholic. A person who has broken the law cannot and will not change until he admits his lawbreaking. If you are not accountable, you are liable to do anything... with consequences to match.

Unaccountable people don't care about how others regard them; therefore they are not constrained by social parameters. While most people worry about having a bad reputation, unaccountable people are only interested in self-preservation. Unaccountable people are dangerous.

Ethical Spring Training as a Corrective "Bubble"

Your early life, if your parents plan it correctly, is a chance to live in somewhat of a protective "bubble" of sorts. It is here, in the home and in educational institutions, where you have the best opportunity to identify and correct weaknesses before you launch your adult life. My own weakness was public speaking.

In college, I would avoid taking classes that had class participation as a part of the grade. But if my dreams of being a trial lawyer were to come true, I would have to learn how to open my mouth in class. I had to face the fear. I hit the fear head on by taking Public Speaking 101. The entire grade was based on six speeches. To combat my shyness and nervousness, I would practice each speech no less than 100 times in front of the mirror. I found out after about the 50th time that I did not need the notes. I memorized the speeches, and delivered them without notes. I only got one A in college and that was in…guess what? Public Speaking 101. Since then, I have never given an opening statement, closing argument or any other speech with notes. They are an unnecessary crutch. Now, memorization is second nature; I never have to refer to my notes during a speech. Exercise the muscle, and you can turn a weakness into a strength. It worked for me; I know it can work for you!

When I taught trial advocacy at Wayne State University School of Law, I made it mandatory that students deliver arguments without notes. They complained endlessly. I told them that practice breeds confidence. I shared with them the story of when my kids were in the first grade and they had Poetry Day. All of the first graders and the parents had to recite a poem. However, the kids had to do it without notes. The parents were more nervous reading their poems than the first graders were reciting theirs. I tell my students, "If a first grader can recite a poem by heart in a room full of adults, why can't a law student memorize an opening and closing argument?" Every year, without fail, the law students deliver passionate arguments without relying on a sheet of paper.

People engage in unethical behavior in part because they fail to acknowledge their weaknesses. Whether your weakness is blaming others, or shyness, or an inability to memorize, you have to be honest with yourself. An unidentified weakness remains a weakness.

In order to identify your weakness, you have to be humble. This is probably one of the most valuable lessons in your ethical spring training. Arrogance is the enemy of ethical leadership. It takes humility to recognize your weakness and it takes courage to correct it.

Our "Better Angels"

Are you faced with an ethical dilemma? Reconnect with your ethical roots! Draw strength from your ethical spring training. Your angel may be a book. It may be a picture or a photograph of you with a coach or a parent. The flashbacks these images generate will put you back in alignment with your true ethical core; keep them visible at home or at work.

Your angel could even be an article of clothing. When my Uncle Genie died, all of his nephews were able to keep one of his ties. I picked a bright red striped tie. My Uncle Genie, a retired high school principal, was beloved by everyone in his hometown of Chesapeake, Virginia. He encouraged everyone. He was kind to everyone. He was a selfless hero. I once heard him say, "When I give you my word, you can take that to the bank." Uncle Genie's brand was reliability. During the summer he would drive to neighboring states and pick up his nephews and bring them back to Virginia to spend quality time fishing on his boat. I once got sick and threw up all over his boat. I later came to learn that my other cousins also got sick on the boat. But Uncle Genie didn't care. He was a kind, unselfish man who believed that cleaning up after his nauseous nephews was a small price to pay for spending good fishing time with them. My Uncle Genie would go out of his way to include us in the activities he loved to do.

Every time I look at or wear that tie, I remember Uncle Genie and his character. Whenever I wear his tie, I am reconnected to his spirit of kindness, unselfishness and dependability. I feel it is a high standard to meet. Uncle Genie played a valuable role in my spring training. I wanted his brand.

Sometimes, simply being in the presence of your "ethical angels" helps. Even if you do not share with them your particular problem, just being around them rubs off. I ran into my kid's high school principal, Glen Shilling, while I was facing a tough ethical decision. I was questioning whether unethical conduct was becoming the "new normal." The principal, like my Uncle Genie, always represented honesty, reliability and compassion. Another selfless hero. I did not share with him the dilemma. I found simply being in his presence helped to solve the problem. His presence reminded me: the new normal is not normal at all. His presence reinforced that unethical conduct is the exception to the rule. His presence reminded me how the sausage can be made. It does not have to be made in a mean spirited, backstabbing, name calling, or cutthroat manner. The principal never subscribed to those tactics; why should I? Sometimes you imitate the ethical traits you see from those you admire without even knowing it. Without saying a word, this principal's presence helped to put me on the right course.

Your angel may not give you specific answers to your dilemma. However, on a few occasions, it will repeat the words of my Chrysler's GPS voice: "You are traveling in an area where turn-by-turn guidance is unavailable; use the directional arrow to guide you." There may not be a person or a rule or policy you can specifically follow. Instead, you have to be guided by your own personal code. Your integrity becomes your "directional arrow." Spring training establishes your directional arrow, and helps you chart an ethical path no matter the situation. The solid ethical foundation provided by "spring training" will lead you to the right destination.

I believe there are ethical angels watching over us. They are rooting for us to do the right thing.

In 2002, I decided to run a marathon. I had never run one before, and I didn't follow the cardinal rule: get enough fluids. It was a hot day, and I collapsed near the 24-mile mark of the 26.2-mile race. The next thing I remember was a lady on the ground next to me handing me cups of water. She kept telling me to drink slowly. She said I had been unconscious for a few minutes. She said I ran a good race, but the Emergency Medical Services' ambulance was on the way. I knew if I got in the EMS truck, I would be disqualified from the race. I told the lady I could finish the race. She replied, "If you are going to run, I will run with you." Amazingly, she jogged with me for about a mile while encouraging me. She ordered me to drink at the next water station. When she saw I was determined to run further and I was relatively OK, she disappeared into the crowd. I went on to finish the race.

To this day, I do not know the name of the person who helped me. She could have left me lying in the street. She could have stayed home that day and not volunteered to help with the marathon. Her aid was a gift from God. It was as if I was touched by an angel. She remains one of my "ethical angels" in the important area of compassion.

I believe as we go through spring training, ethical angels become more visible. They run next to you, trail behind you, and dash ahead of you. If you fall, they will provide aid. They provide the framework upon which you will make ethical decisions. They provide your ethical boundaries. They provide your definition of what is right and what is wrong. They are the inspiration for you to be an angel to others. They provide the strength for you to run the race of your life.

Ethical values can be mixed just like colors. You know how you mix primary colors in different combinations to create a whole rainbow. You can mix ethical values in the same way. For example:

Honesty + Consistency = Integrity
Generosity + Humility = Empathy
Consistency + Encouragement = Empowerment

The primary ethical values should be taught in spring training. You should not leave spring training without practicing these traits over and over again. The core primary ethical values produce secondary ethical values that will benefit you throughout life. Later in life, you will be able to act with integrity because the values of honesty and consistency were drilled into your head. Later in life, you will have empathy because generosity and humility were treasured values during your spring training. Later, you will be able to uplift, enhance and empower others to reach greatness because consistent encouragement was given to you during your spring training. Ethical leadership starts with you knowing and claiming your core values.

PRACTICE TIP

Draw an ethical tree. The roots of the tree should include your ethical ancestors and role models. The trunk of your tree represents your personal experiences and lessons learned that have shaped your ethical code. The trunk grows another ring every year. The branches should include the lives you have impacted with your ethical brand. The leaves are the people that have been influenced by the people you have touched.

CHAPTER TWO
Play Ball

Spring training is over. There are no more scrimmages or practice games. The preseason is over. Now is the time for competitive play. The games count. Now is the time to officially "play ball." "Play ball" is the first day of a new job. Whether that job is your first or your last, those first days count more than any others. My predecessor at the United States Attorneys' Office, Saul Green, put it this way: "It takes courage to walk through the door."

How do you walk through the door? You walk through the door with a solid ethical foundation. You walk through the door armed with confidence that you can be a positive instrument of change.

Once you get settled into the position, you may see a variety of ethical characters. You may see Slicksters, Enablers, Cynics and Super Heroes. Your effectiveness in managing these relationships with these characters will determine your success.

The Slickster

"Slick" is the ability to accomplish unethical goals without detection. Slicksters are treacherous. Slicksters revel in the double-cross. The Slickster finds inspiration in deception; they enjoy gaming the system. They are often very intelligent, but sadly refuse to use their talents for good.

A Slickster may pad the hours on their time sheet, use the company credit card for personal use, or reveal confidential information to a competitor. Slicksters have no allegiance to the institution. Their only concern is self-interest - a get-over mentality.

It is important that every institution have checks and balances that expose Slicksters. Frequent routine audits of productivity, clear lines of oversight responsibility and defined ethical expectations will facilitate Slickster detection. However, in many cases, the Slickster has become skillful at avoiding discovery. The Slickster may be so clever that it takes investigators years to uncover the misdeeds. Just like the cheating tournament tennis player, the Slickster does not have a guilty conscience. The Slickster can be motivated to achieve a more ethical brand if that brand serves his self-interest. Gone unchecked, a Slickster is a cancer to the company; an ethical leader must take affirmative steps to prevent the cancer from spreading throughout the organization. The leadership sets the tone or else the Slickster continues to profit from his self-interest. Slicksters should be called to the carpet. With rare exception, they should be removed from the organization.

A lifetime of good work can be wiped away by a single unethical act. It can all come crashing down very fast. Once the improper act is committed, you cannot take it back. You cannot un-ring the bell. The Slickster fails to truly appreciate the power of motivating others or the value of repairing the flaws in a system. If the Slickster would put their own unique talents to good use, they would move to higher ethical ground. If the Slickster worked for the common good instead of self-interest, they never would press the unethical "send" button. Typically though, we cannot count on the Slickster to check himself. Tragically, their talent is misdirected until they are led to a better place. It is the role of the ethical leader to change the culture to reward the Slickster for doing the right thing.

I have seen brilliant people get derailed by unethical conduct. Many are visionaries who could have a tremendous positive impact on society. They are smart and hardworking, but lack an ethical compass. In retrospect, people often realize too late that they did not have to swindle others to capitalize on their brilliance. The slickness was not worth it. The deceptive practice ultimately leads to their downfall. In the end, the corruption becomes their brand.

The Enabler

Enablers do not stand on principle. The Enabler feeds the beast. The Enabler adapts to the ethical code of the leader. To promote their self-interest, they give the leader only what the leader wants to hear. Enablers rarely disagree with the decision maker even if they know it is wrong. The enabler will ask, "If no one else is doing the right thing, why should we?" Enablers know the leader's deficiencies, but look the other way. If the boss says jump, the enabler says, “How high?” The Enabler, in her failure to take the lead, never asks, “Should we jump at all?”

The Cynic

Cynics, unlike Slicksters and Enablers, do not actively support an unethical culture. But, because Cynics are highly skeptical, their pessimistic perspective creates a feeling that the culture cannot change so don't bother to push for a more ethical workplace. They have been burned in the past and they discourage others from believing that they have the power to make a difference. Cynics have given up hope that positive change can occur.

The good news is that Cynics, like Enablers, can be rehabilitated. Once again, a change in leadership philosophy will produce better results. The trust of the Cynic can be regained once unethical behavior is eliminated. Cynics need to know the organization has zero tolerance for improper conduct. If the organization, through its leadership, displays real, tangible examples of positive ethical change, the Cynic can be shown the road to recovery. Connecting ethics to action is key.

To effectively work in an environment with such a diverse assortment of ethical characters takes a large dosage of tenacity and determination. It takes patience and compassion. It takes the full spectrum of “colors” in the ethical color wheel.

In short, it takes a Super Hero.

The Super Hero

Super Heroes are truly committed to doing the right thing for the right reason, time and time again. Super Heroes are committed to doing what's in the best interest of the organization. They have no hidden agendas. Super Heroes have pure motives. Their loyalty is to advancing the greater good, not to their own self-interest. Ethical Super Heroes are offended by unfairness. They often go unnoticed because of their humility. They may be scattered throughout the organization. Many are simply waiting for the opportunity to uncork their talents.

Years ago, I had a golden retriever named Max. One day I was walking Max and I noticed a mixed breed puppy walking toward us. I walked across the street in an attempt to avoid the stray mutt, but he followed us across the street. Max and I then opted to go the opposite direction, assuming this puppy would not venture off the block. The puppy followed us around the corner. We could not shake him. He was like glue and stayed with us the entire walk of about eight blocks. This tenacious pup followed us home right up the driveway and through the back door of the house. He ended up staying seven years. I named the dog Buddy and he became a big part of our family. He was the only dog that I know that was prescribed a root canal for a bad tooth and I happily paid for it because he was such a good friend. The character of Buddy is one of courageous determination. He was determined to find a family. He would cross streets and go down strange blocks. He would not be denied. He was our shadow.

Dogged determination is what drives a Super Hero. The Super Hero is a constant voice of change. They remain vigilant even if muzzled by the company. The Super Hero keeps pushing and pressing the issue. They are not intimidated by environments that frown upon debate and deny change-agents. They are not deceived by the Slicksters, not deterred by the eager Enablers or the pessimism of the Cynics. The ethical Super Hero tries to promote an environment that is not governed by fear. The Super Hero strives to change the conversation. The Super Hero gets the entire team to rally behind ethical leadership.

Ethical leadership is doing the right thing for the right reason time and time again. The Super Hero steers the conversation towards what is in the best interest of the organization, not what is in anyone's personal best interest. They do not wait for others to do the right thing. If it is the right thing to do, the Super Hero simply does it. If the organization is suffering from a financial crisis and pay cuts must be made, the Super Hero personally takes the cut without asking who else is taking the cut. Nor does the Super Hero say, "I will take the cut once someone else takes the cut." Super Heroes lead by example.

For fourteen years my wife and I have served as directors of the summer youth camp at our church in Detroit. The camping ministry has taken as many as eighty youngsters under 18 years of age to an overnight campsite for five nights and four days of activities. My principal responsibility is to motivate the reluctant campers and counselors to participate in calisthenics. Each camp day starts with a 6:00 a.m. (not 6:01 a.m.) workout. When the schedule is announced, the cynics and naysayers come out of the woodwork. The excuses flow like a river. If looks could kill, I would be a dead man! I explain that no one else their age is up at 6:00 in the morning working out and the discipline learned will spill over into their school life. I explain the early morning workout makes them special. "If you can run at 6:00 a.m.," I tell them, "you can study at 6:00 a.m."

By my raising the bar, the kids respond. No one wants to be the last one to the workout. The early morning camp workout becomes a source of pride. By the end of the week, the campers are beating me to the workout. Cynics are turned into believers when there is no compromising on the workout time and effort. A solid work ethic is the backbone of an effective ethical leader. An ethical leader takes no pride in taking shortcuts. Ethical leaders take pride in the daily effort of doing the right thing the right way every time.

The Super Hero steers Cynics, Enablers and Slicksters away from rationalizing unethical behavior. They obliterate the "everybody is doing it" argument. The Super Hero recognizes that a history of wrong conduct by others does not give people a free pass to continue going the wrong way.

The Super Hero recognizes that no decision is too small or insignificant not to have ethical ramifications and is alert to the gradual erosion of ethics through minor transgressions. The ethical Super Hero could be in a grocery store. The sign says "Express Checkout, 10 items or less." The Superhero may have 15 items in his cart. The Super Hero will not rationalize by saying that the three cans of pop is "really just one item." Today it could be 15 items and next week you would feel justified jumping in the Express Checkout with 20 items.

The Super Hero avoids the slippery slope of incremental ethical missteps by never getting on the slope. The Super Hero believes there is no such thing as a victimless crime. Even if no one else is in the Express Checkout line, you weaken your ethical code by breaking the rules. In essence, you become a victim of your own wrongdoing and are now more susceptible to future ethical missteps.

I was fortunate to be one of the lawyers that represented Major League Baseball in a steroid investigation conducted by former United States Senator George Mitchell. In my view, the

Super Heroes of the investigation were all of the players that refused to compromise the integrity of the game and declined to use steroids to their own personal detriment.

The players who did not use steroids were innocent victims. The excuse of "it's the culture" or "everyone is doing it" did not resonate with those ethically stronger players. The benefits of quicker recovery from injuries or the ability to hit a ball farther or pitch a ball faster did not alter the moral compass of the players who did not use steroids. Despite the risk of earning less money than the steroid user, the ethical ballplayers drew a line in the sand and refused to cross it. These Super Heroes were individuals that would rise or fall the old-fashioned way, through hard work. They did not want their brand and years of hard work tainted by being associated with steroids. Making the team or getting a lucrative contract or winning the game through deception was simply not worth it. They had the ethical fortitude not to be governed by short-term advantage.

Many players felt they could "out slick" the system and not get caught. If they were questioned about steroid use, they would deny it. The reputations of these Slicksters will be forever tarnished. There were also a number of Enablers milking the system. These Enablers, knowing that steroid use was not allowed, profited by distributing and in some instances injecting steroids into professional athletes. The Cynic believes that everyone is cheating. It is only when there is swift and certain punishment that the Cynic regains his confidence in the purity of the game.

Ethical leaders, like ethical athletes, must be prepared to stick to their principles even if it puts them at a competitive disadvantage. Public servants, for example, are prohibited from campaigning during work hours and on work property. Public servants are also prohibited from using government equipment for political purposes. These rules apply even if it puts a candidate at a competitive disadvantage. It is important that there be clear rules that prevent the mixing of politics and work. Loose enforcement of the rules enables the Slickster. Strict enforcement of the rules helps to regain the confidence of the Cynic, keeps the Slickster at bay, and nullifies the Enabler because they have no one to enable. Nowhere would these principles be tested more than when I was asked to become second- in-charge at the County of Wayne, the largest county in Michigan. I was appointed Deputy Wayne County Executive after a major scandal hit the press. I would have to bring everything I had learned about ethics to bear on this assignment.

My first order of business when I became Deputy Wayne County Executive was to evaluate whether there was an effective, understandable and precise ethics policy. When I accepted the position, the County was embroiled in controversy. At the heart of the controversy was a lucrative severance payment a County employee received upon leaving the job. In addition, the same employee was highly compensated for serving on a county-related board. On top of these issues, there was a pending federal criminal investigation and several lawsuits alleging misconduct.

I had walked into a hurricane.

People who followed the story in the news often ask, "How do you change the culture of Wayne County?" My answer is always, "It's like eating an elephant; you tackle it one bite at a time." My first "bite" was improving and executing a new ethics policy.

I had to hit the problems head on, first establishing a new policy that expressly prohibited employees from being paid when they served on a county related board. No ambiguity there! I put some specific checks and balances in place as well. Any retirement benefit change had to go through four layers of internal approvals. In addition, before any change would go into effect, two external entities had to be notified: the Wayne County Commission and the Wayne County Retirement Commission. The new ethics policy also prohibited any employee from being directed to participate in any political activity by a supervisor. Violation of the new ethics policy would result in mandatory discipline. The new policy promoted transparency and put sufficient checks in the process so that these kinds of activities will be much easier to spot, correct and deter.

Wayne County Executive Robert Ficano gave me the green light to revamp this policy. That brings up another key point: Real ethical change comes from the top; management must be supportive if such change is to work. Too often, management hunkers down and fails to acknowledge the need for improvement. They take on an "us" versus "them" mentality which prevents honest reflection and change.

For approximately six weeks I would bring my work product to the Executive Management team for discussion. I kept them fully informed of my research. I sought and invited feedback from inside and outside of the organization. I distributed weekly drafts to make people comfortable with the changes. There would be no surprises.

With the ethics policy, I adopted a management style of "power to, not power over." Staff was empowered to react to the proposed changes and provide meaningful input. I respected the feedback and incorporated many of the suggestions into the new policy. Staff would be similarly part of the ethical processes built into the new policy. By being inclusive and not ramming the policy down the throats of the impacted staff, I was seeking "buy-in."

If the policy was going to be respected, the process in establishing the policy had to be fair. A dictatorial approach where the new policy was announced without any input would only trigger resentment and pushback. A "win" in achieving a new ethics policy would not be a win if there was no buying into the process. Finally, transparency meant that everyone could see what was going on, that everyone would be free to share their ethical concerns based on clearer, more specific guidelines. I felt that by working together, the entire team could bring about real effective change.

Of course, when the policy was rolled out, there were doubters. Instead of saying the policy was a step in the right direction, some cynics declared it was "too little too late."

I did not get discouraged. Having the courage to stand up for what you believe is a key trait of ethical leadership. I continued to make ethics a top priority. I continually asked—and directed everyone who worked with me to ask—"What is the ethical impact of our decisions?" I conducted training on Ethical Leadership. The training kicked off with a definition of Ethical Leadership. I defined Ethical Leadership as "doing the right thing for the right reason, time and time again." Ethics is now a topic that is openly discussed. It is not a topic that is swept under the rug. With overall input and buy-in, a revamped policy, and ongoing open discussions, we now have taken several bites out of the elephant!

One of the biggest projects in the State was the construction of the Wayne County Jail. It was fraught with controversy and has been a sore spot for the Administration. But after we implemented the new ethics policy, my colleagues began asking a different question, one they were not asking when I walked through the door. In deciding whether to scrap the project and rehab the current jails or to move the project to another location, my colleagues were now asking, "What is the right thing to do?" This ethics question was unprompted and unsolicited. The conversation and the brand were slowly starting to change.

While the ethics policy was adopted without resistance, another issue that hit closer to the pocketbook took more persistence to implement. I used the dogged determination that I learned from my dog, Buddy, to win this issue.

Prior to my arrival, the Executive Branch instituted a 10% employee compensation cut. In addition, a mileage allowance was eliminated for the vast majority of employees…but not all. The problem was that those still eligible to receive a mileage allowance were in essence taking only a 5% compensation cut.

I recognized the flaw. The issue was impacting the pocketbook of a large group of people. I continually brought the issue up week after week for what seemed like months. I was inclusive and sought feedback. The process was exhausting. I could not get an answer. Avoidance is a common technique when dealing with ethical issues. The ostrich approach to solving ethical problems can be very frustrating. Avoidance can be code for "no." I felt the issue would die if I did not keep bringing it up. The Administration had its head stuck in the sand and I was not having success getting it out. I felt like I was running headway into a brick wall, and I had to make a decision.

The frustration became so intense I had decided to quit if the loophole was not corrected at our next Executive Management meeting. I felt if the Administration could not correct an obvious flaw on a relatively minor issue, we'd never be able to tackle the major issues that faced the County.

At what would have been my last Executive Management meeting if the change had not been made, I decided to frame the issue as an ethical issue, not a budget issue. I argued it was unfair for our employees who were not eligible for the mileage allowance to shoulder the entire 10% compensation cut. The unequal treatment was unethical. Also, eliminated means just that: eliminated. Once the mileage allowance was eliminated, it could not be applied as an offset to compensation. Framed in this manner, the CEO approved my recommendation, correcting the payment inequity.

I was so elated that I went for a victory lap. I had my gym clothes in the car and had planned to run after work in the evening, but I couldn't wait. On my lunch hour I changed and went for a great run in celebration of the Administration doing the right thing. Pay equity: another bite out of the elephant.

Then, I had to take another bite: addressing morale. When I arrived at Wayne County many people felt suffocated. A suffocating work environment does not produce good results. People cannot relax. They feel they are walking on eggshells. They are hesitant to express an opinion.

I tried to change the atmosphere by embracing the power of encouragement. I sent letters of praise and appreciation to employees' homes. At staff meetings I highlighted the accomplishments of every department. I regularly sent emails to congratulate and recognize employees. It is easy to complain. It is easier to destroy a ship than it is to build a ship. Encouragement is a key building material. I use it liberally.

Ethical leaders should equip staff with the tools necessary to do the right thing. Employees equipped with a positive attitude are more likely to produce good results. Ethical leaders play a major role in shaping the attitude of employees. What may seem insignificant can have a huge impact on morale.

I noticed in one location there were no nameplates on the office doors of County employees. I was told this was the case because employees were told they would not be there long enough to justify buying a nameplate. The "no nameplate" rule served as a reminder that you were expendable. It promoted a "ruling by fear" management style.

A nameplate recognizes your individuality and territory. It also serves as the organization's validation of you and your position. The nameplate helps to create buy-in. The reason for the "no nameplate" policy made office morale a nonexistent priority.

This was an easy fix. The ordering of the nameplate itself was a small bite out of the elephant. What the nameplate represented was a substantial bite.

Accumulating Ethical Deficits

Just as an administration can have an accumulated budget deficit, it can also have an accumulated "ethical deficit." An accumulated budget deficit is a carryover debt from a previous accounting period. It is a loss a company keeps on its books from one accounting period to the next. If it continues very long, the company will not survive. If the company continues to suffer losses year after year, selling the company or filing for bankruptcy protection become real options.

The organization must take tangible steps to avert an accumulated budget deficit. It must identify the factors causing the deficit and take action to prevent those same factors from continuing to have a negative influence on the financial viability of the organization.

Likewise, an organization can have an accumulated ethical deficit. This is an ethical debt that is carried over from previous years. Compensation packages that favor a few individuals and not the organization as a whole cause an accumulated ethical deficit. Nepotism can add to an accumulated ethical deficit. Not treating "like people alike" adds to the ethical deficit. The failure to apply rules equally creates a group of exempt employees. Policies that protect these "untouchables" add to the ethical deficit. A culture of putting self-interest ahead of the public interest is the dominant factor causing the ethical deficit.

Nothing bankrupts the morale of an organization more than management turning a blind eye to an accumulated ethical deficit. An organization may not survive if it fails to take aggressive steps to avert an accumulated ethical deficit. People will be there physically but will check out mentally. They will not go the extra mile. There is no loyalty. There is no trust. The organization will leak like a sieve. If the company repeats the same mistakes of previous years and the unethical decisions outnumber the ethical decisions, then the organization is adding to the ethical deficit. An organization can drown under the weight of an accumulated ethical deficit.

To eliminate an ethical deficit takes bold and decisive leadership. Fortunately, an ethical deficit can turn into an ethical surplus if management embraces the definition of ethical leadership and repeatedly does the right thing for the right reason. This means ethics does not go on vacation. There are no days off. There is no decision that is so small not to have ethical implications. The "no days off" rule reminds me of a running group I have been a part of for over twenty-five years.

I run with a group of neighbors at 5 a.m. three days a week. We run all year round. We have run in every known weather condition. Rain, snow, ice or the heat have not deterred us from running together. There are no days off. You can count the times on one hand that someone in the group has missed a running day. These are the most dedicated people I have ever known. The group has earned a brand of dependability and durability.

We welcome anyone who has the discipline and the desire to join us. However, we place all newcomers on probation. Neophytes have to come on time for two straight weeks. Once they pass the two-week test, they are officially a member of the group. There have been many well-intentioned runners who have violated probation.

Likewise, a culture will not be changed with a single ethical victory. It requires a sustained commitment of trying to do the right thing. The right thing does not mean being perfect but it does require you to repeatedly connect ethics to action. To get off ethical probation you must consistently make sound ethical decisions. In essence we become what we practice. Individuals and companies can become ethical by practicing ethical behavior.

When ethics fails to go on vacation and does not take any sick or personal days off, an ethical surplus is created. The goal is to create a surplus. Making sound ethical decisions day after day, month after month, and year after year builds a surplus. The surplus will become your ethical brand.

PRACTICE TIP

There are 3 keys to hitting a good serve in tennis. Tennis players should visualize the following:

1. Scratching your back (bending your elbow)
2. Swatting the fly (snap the wrist)
3. Sweeping the floor (follow through)

Apply the keys to hitting a good serve to changing an ethical culture:

1. Scratch the back (bend the elbow of the culture by fighting for change)

2. Swat the fly (attack the culture with clear ethical rules)

3. Sweep the floor (strict enforcement of the ethical rules)

CHAPTER THREE

Bring Your Glove

When my son was about ten years old, we went to a Detroit Tigers baseball game. As I was backing out of the driveway he yelled, "Stop, I forgot my glove." I said, "Why do you need your glove? We are not going to your game; we are going to the Tigers' game." He said, "I need my glove in case they hit me a foul ball." I stopped the car and he ran into the house and got his glove.

In the mind of a ten year old, what does this glove symbolize? It symbolizes hope. It symbolizes faith. There could be fifty thousand people at the game; probably only a 1 in 50,000 chance a foul ball would come my son's way. Despite the odds, my son always took his glove to the game because from his perspective, the cup of life is not half empty, it is half full.

Ethical leaders always carry their glove. Ethical leaders expect good things to happen despite the odds of success. They know they can be the one to make a difference. Nearly a half century ago, Mahatma Gandhi said, "You must BE the change you want to see in the world."

As you experience new challenges, take your glove with you! No matter where you are in life, entering college, entering grade school or entering the workforce, plan to learn how to make a difference. The motto of Bethune- Cookman University, "Enter to Learn, Exit to Serve" is an expectation we should all have to become ethical leaders. Expect a smooth transition. Expect to change the world. When you start a new job, expect to make an impact. Expect that your work will be recognized and rewarded. Expect that you will do the "right thing." Expect to be able to get along with your colleagues.

When my daughter was twelve, she was invited to play with a rival team at the national AAU basketball tournament in Springfield, Missouri. Her AAU team did not qualify that year so a rival team asked if she could play with them. If she accepted the invitation, she would have been the only African American on the team. Negative influence comes in different voices. A friend left a message on our answering machine encouraging her not to go because he feared that someone on the team would say or do something racially insensitive and that would make for a negative experience. Even though I was fully aware of the racial makeup of the rival team, I strongly disagreed with the caller.

I encouraged my daughter to take her glove with her on the trip. "Expect things to go well," I told her. "If something is said or done that is questionable, don't assume the worst. Be determined to gain something positive from the trip."

As it turned out, it was a great trip. My daughter made some terrific friends, and the basketball became secondary. As a matter of fact, many of the players on the rival team would later join her AAU team. She was, in the parlance of author Malcolm Gladwell, a "Connector." In her own unassuming way she became a bridge builder because she "took her glove." She opened up new worlds for both her old and new teammates, and decimated the arguments of her naysayers.

Having the courage to step out on faith, whether it is pursuing a new job or presenting a new idea which goes against conventional design, requires a firm grasp of the glove. Life then becomes a self-fulfilling prophecy. It works in sports as well as life. Most tennis matches are won or lost before the match starts. The player that thinks they are going to win will win most of the time. Danger comes when we stop bringing the glove. This means we stop dreaming. We stop expecting something better.

Don't accept the views of negative influences, critics or dream-killers. Even if you don't catch the foul ball this time, you should still bring the glove to the next game. Even if you lose a match point in tennis, still bring the glove! We don't fail by dreaming. We fail by not having a dream.

Ethical leaders have faith that goodness resides in all of us. There is a presumption of goodness. Despite the past, the ethical leader believes that people, once properly directed, will do the right thing.

I remember being the keynote speaker at a black tie banquet where the audience was mostly white. The gentleman who introduced me had heard me speak before. He was familiar with my speaking style. Right before he handed me the microphone, he whispered something disturbing in my ear. He said, "Don't start preaching to these white folks." I was disturbed because I only know one way to give a speech, and that is with heart and passion. I felt if the banquet committee was either embarrassed or concerned about "preaching" they should not have invited me. My speaking repertoire has only one pitch, and that's a fastball. I do not have a curve ball or a changeup. I am going to throw the fastball no matter who is up to bat. I do not adjust my style to suit the audience; to do so would show a lack of sincerity. People know when you are phony. It's like the Gong Show, where the audience will shut you out when they smell snake oil. The audience will keep you on a short leash and will snatch it if you are not genuine and sincere. You must be comfortable with yourself. This allows you to throw the pitch you have the innate ability to throw. Having faith that the message would resonate, no matter how it was delivered, gave me confidence to speak with conviction.

My "preaching" did not offend. I believe the speech was well received because it was spoken from the heart.

I had a similar experience later—but this time it was with a largely African American audience. When I was running for the Michigan Supreme Court, I was invited to speak at a NAACP Freedom Fund dinner about three hours from my home. The organizers were excited that I was coming. They told me to arrive early in the day because there was a parade before the dinner and they wanted me to be the Grand Marshal. "The mayor will give you a key to the city and introduce you to all of the city officials at the parade," they told me. I was looking forward to the entire day. My wife and our two young kids at the time packed the car and left at the crack of dawn. When we arrived, I was met at the hotel by the organizer who explained there had been a change in plans.

"What is the change?" I asked.

He explained. "We didn't know at the time that you were nominated by the Republican Party to run for the Supreme Court." He said I was no longer the Grand Marshal of the parade and I would not get a key to the city. "The only reason you're still speaking at the banquet was because we did not have time to find a new speaker," he explained. Clearly, the group had succumbed to naysayers, which allowed them to judge me before they met me.

At the dinner, I once again spoke from the heart on family, faith and community. It was essentially the same speech I had given at the black tie affair. The speech received the same positive reaction. The apologies came from everywhere. The mayor asked if I could come back tomorrow because he would then give me the key to the city. The organizers said they had no idea the message would be so powerful and penetrating. Although I lost the Michigan Supreme Court election, that night was a major victory. Preconceived views and misconceptions were broken down, and I found a way to build more bridges. You can lose the battle and win the ethical war.

You must be true to yourself.

A few months after the election, I was fortunate to be appointed to the Michigan Court of Appeals. I was happy to see at my swearing-in ceremony my host from the Freedom Fund dinner. He returned the favor by driving three hours to attend the ceremony. We had come full circle. Thankfully, he crossed the bridge I built.

These life lessons in faith helped a great deal as I stepped into the position of the United States Attorney for the Eastern District of Michigan. Having confidence to bring my glove and to throw my pitch, I was ready.

The year was 2001. I had just been named United States Attorney for the Eastern District of Michigan. It was obviously one of the toughest times we faced as a nation. Imad Hamad, then-Director of the American-Arab Anti-Discrimination Committee (ADC), was working hard to stop racial profiling of the Arab community by law enforcement officials. He was an important voice who spoke on behalf of the approximately 200,000 persons of Middle Eastern descent who live in Metropolitan Detroit—a higher concentration than in any other part of the country. Two years before, he had been honored in the U.S. Congressional Record for his anti-discrimination efforts—"his tireless efforts to… eradicate discrimination against Americans of Arab descent. "

At the time, Hamad was on his way to a meeting in Washington, D.C. He was concerned about racial profiling in a major airport hub in Amsterdam. Northwest Airlines was partnering with KLM, the Amsterdam- based airline, to operate the Amsterdam hub, and Hamad found himself in the middle of two behemoths—really, three—who were all blaming each other. Northwest said they were following KLM's lead in their screening policies, and KLM's private security company said that they were merely following U.S. Immigration policy. They all agreed to meet at the Northwest/KLM hub in Washington.

The date: September 11, 2001. Hamad was literally in the air at the time of the tragic attacks on U.S. soil.

"As we're in the sky," remembered Hamad, the captain said, "we have been directed to land at Dulles instead of Reagan National Airport. No one thought it was a big deal at the time."

The plane landed, and then the captain said: "Our nation has been the victim of a terrorist attack." Hamad remembered: "Then they all started looking at me."

The meeting was canceled. Hamad had to stay in D.C. for a week, then came back to Michigan. He found himself in D.C. a few days later, in the national ADC office. The Detroit ADC office called him and said that the FBI wanted to talk to people of Arab descent— citizens and non-citizens alike. Hamad called the Detroit FBI head John Bell and met with him. Bell explained the unprecedented nature of the situation.

"We know people are afraid," he said. "We want to work with you." Hamad responded, "As much as people are afraid, they are also hesitant to trust you." He and Bell agreed to work together to address the dual problem of investigating the attacks and cultivating the trust of the Arab community, which previously had not found much reason to trust the government.

Hamad praised Congressman John Conyers, Congressman John Dingell, and Senator Carl Levin for pledging their support in the effort. Senator Levin urged Hamad to call me. According to Hamad, Senator Levin said, "We've just nominated and approved Jeff Collins, just call him now. He hasn't started yet, but he is a man of integrity."

Hamad followed Levin's recommendation and called me. My first question to him was "How can I help you?"

The best way to gain the trust of someone is to offer yourself

I had a major position, but in the end government officials are, most importantly, servants of the people. I wanted Hamad to know that I saw myself that way. We had our first meeting, and invited organizations like the NAACP and the American Civil Liberties Union to the table, as well as other active community members. The first thing to do was to have a dialogue and begin a conversation. "We need to have regular meetings so that we can understand each other," I explained. I knew that would be important.

None of us had any idea where this would lead. But we knew this: we didn't want our differences to keep us apart. We needed to establish a human bond. Even though we knew we'd disagree on some things, we also knew that those disagreements could in no way block meaningful dialogue.

The pushback was immediate. Both Hamad and I were criticized by our supporters as well as our detractors. Some saluted Hamad; others called him a "sellout." The Arab community was concerned. They were suspicious of the idea of government-community "dialogue." Some called it merely another public relations scam, a way to allow people to vent without seeing any real change. Others said that Hamad was an informant.

As the meetings progressed, many—on both sides—began to see things differently. But the resulting initiative was a major step in bringing the community together, while still allowing the government to do its job of securing public safety.

As the meetings progressed, we began to talk about what to name this unlikely group of government officials and citizens. As I thought about it, I began to consider what bridges do. Bridges link two separate bodies of land together, so that people can move smoothly back and forth. They allow for people on one side of the water to meet with people on the other side. "BRIDGES" would be the perfect acronym, I thought:

Building **R**espect **I**n **D**iverse **G**roups to **E**nhance **S**ensitivity

The group liked the name, and BRIDGES was formed. Hamad and I established BRIDGES first in Detroit, and then traveled throughout the State of Michigan to push this notion of citizen dialogue with government.

Law enforcement was able to hear the concerns, complaints and frustrations of the community. The community representatives were able to hear firsthand the policies and perspective of the government. Through monthly meetings, trust was enhanced. We were creating an environment where neither the federal law enforcement community nor the Middle Eastern Community was viewed as the enemy; instead we viewed each other as allies. A collaborative approach to public safety protects the community. Our partnership was put to the test with the Department of Justice Interview Project.

Shortly after 9/11, every federal prosecutor's office was given a list of people to interview. The people interviewed were not suspects. It was hoped that the people interviewed might have information that could assist law enforcement in preventing another terrorist attack. My district had the largest interview list in the country.

We decided to do something different. Instead of having federal agents show up unannounced at people's doors; we decided to send out a letter. The letter asked the person to contact our office and set up a time and location for the interview. The letter indicated that the interview was voluntary. The letter emphasized in a boldface sentence that the government had no reason to believe the people being interviewed were, in any way, associated with terrorist activities.

The simple act of sending a letter gave the recipients, who were not suspected of having done anything wrong, a sense of respect. As it turned out, our district conducted well over 300 interviews. The response rate was greater than any other office assigned more than 200 interviews. The success was due in large part to members of BRIDGES allaying community fears and anxieties about the initiative. A report issued by the Migration Policy Institute (MPI) cited the interview project in our District as exemplary and recommended that similar procedures be followed in other Districts should a similar mandate be issued. Today, that letter sits in the Arab American Museum of History in Dearborn, Michigan.

To make BRIDGES work, both Imad Hamad and I had to carry our gloves. Many expected the partnership not to work. Some critics felt that traditional law enforcement efforts should be focused solely on investigating and prosecuting cases in court. Others did not see the benefits of community policing. Make no mistake: even internally, I had pushback. There were people in the Justice Department that called me "soft" for facilitating these dialogues. Too "touchy-feely," they would say.

But I felt differently. Throughout my life, I experienced the benefits of diversity. I attended Friends School in Detroit for six years. The mission of the school was that "goodness" resided in every child. The goodness transcended color, class and culture. I could see the mission of Friends School in the operation of BRIDGES.

As a college student at Northwestern University, I was surprised to see a campus that was segregated by choice. Students of different ethnic backgrounds would not eat together and would rarely socialize together. I felt students fumbled a golden opportunity to appreciate the beauty of diversity. I was determined not to let law enforcement fumble an opportunity to reach out to a vulnerable community.

Instead of feeding into anti-Arab sentiment which surrounded us after 9/11, we found a more moral position for the win-win. Our model of working together received national recognition. BRIDGES still exists after twelve years and is still described as the gold standard of government and community partnerships. In fact, the Department of Homeland Security's Office of Civil Rights began establishing "roundtable discussions" that looked a lot like our BRIDGES meetings—a testament to our mutual commitment to work in collaboration, uncover all views and concerns, and address what seemed to be mutually exclusive goals in an innovative way characterized by the gold standard of government service: RESPECT.

The horrific events of 9/11 tested the core values of our country. Civil libertarians argued the Department of Justice response to 9/11 went too far. Others argued there would be no civil liberties left to protect without aggressive law enforcement policies. I walked a tightrope between these competing interests.

I remember speaking at a Dr. Martin Luther King Jr. holiday event at the University of Michigan Law School. The very topic was balancing national security and civil liberties. During the question and answer part of the program, I was provided a live example of the topic.

With a soft trembling voice, a female audience member explained the ordeal of her husband. Her husband had been taken into custody by immigration officials over a month ago. She had not seen nor heard from him since. No phone calls, no visits, no letters. She was worried sick. She feared the worst. She wanted to speak to him.

I was moved by her plea for help. I told her I would find out where her husband was being detained and I would arrange a phone call between the two of them.

After I volunteered to help, I was told by the organizers of the event, it was as if the "red sea" came together. To me it was a simple human gesture. I had a flashback to the second day on the job when I participated in another Town Hall meeting. The topic was combating discriminatory backlash post 9/11. Emotions in the Arab American community were raw. An angry audience member yelled at the government representatives for what he believed was "profiling." A high-ranking official of the Department of Justice yelled back at the person. This was a classic lesson in how not to handle a conflict. The meeting deteriorated into a shouting match. From that heated exchange I came to appreciate those who have a gift in calming and not escalating conflict.

When someone is disrespectful to you, the knee-jerk reaction is to return the favor. However the ethical leader rises above the acrimony and reflects on the source of the others person's anger. Why are they so upset and frustrated? Can you see the problem through their lens? You can acknowledge the pain of an angry audience member without compromising your position. Just listening is an important step in resolving a conflict. Listening without interrupting is a form of respect.

At the University of Michigan Law School, just listening to the wife, who had lost total contact with her imprisoned spouse, helped to calm the waters. The next step was following through. If you want ethics to be your brand, you must be prepared to keep your promises.

I found out her husband was Rabih Haddad. Mr. Haddad was a Muslim cleric living in Ann Arbor, Michigan. He was a community activist and raised funds for Islamic charities. On the day he was taken into custody, a charity he co-founded in Chicago was shut down. Government investigators questioned whether these charities had links to terrorism. Mr. Haddad was not charged with a crime. He was taken into custody for overstaying his tourist visa. After Mr. Haddad was taken from his home in Ann Arbor, he was detained in Chicago.

I called my colleague, the United States Attorney in Chicago, Patrick Fitzgerald, and he was very helpful in facilitating the phone call. Mrs. Haddad thanked me for the phone call. The phone call did not compromise national security and it allowed a wife the human decency of being able to talk to her jailed spouse.

Whether it is arranging a phone call or sending ethnic interview letters, doing the right thing can be a simple act. The simple acts can have big consequences. Simple acts of kindness and consideration of others done over and over again can become your brand.

There are no law school courses in diplomacy. You do not need a formal education to be equipped to do the right thing. What I learned most from all of the community outreach work with the Middle Eastern community was "seek first to understand, then to be understood."

PRACTICE TIP

Expand your cultural comfort zone. It is important for ethical leaders to be culturally sensitive. Try new experiences. Heighten your cultural awareness. Visit ethnic museums, or go to concerts of musicians and groups that you might not normally attend. Read books written by people of other cultures. As you do this, you will undoubtedly recognize core values common to human beings—the best way to expand your "zone"!

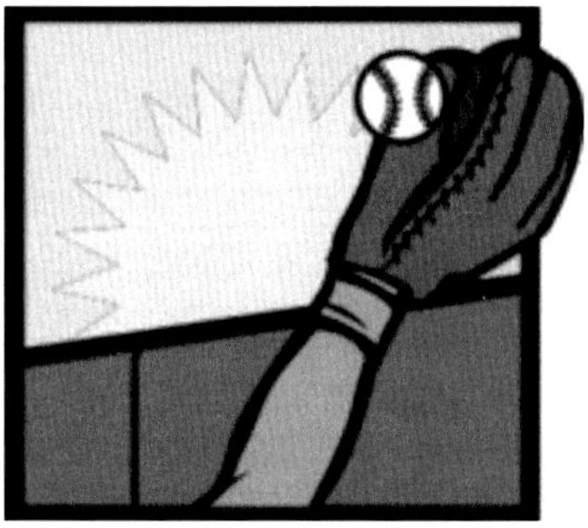

CHAPTER FOUR

Block The Plate

***A**s the runner came charging around third base, the outfielder picked up the ball and fired it to home plate. The job of the catcher is to block the plate. It is imperative that the catcher protect home base to prevent the runner from scoring. The catcher was braced for impact and a collision. The catcher had resolved to sacrifice his body for the team. To score, the base runner will have to get around the catcher's block of home base.*

Good catchers, like good executives, must protect the plate.

The question I raise is: What is your plate? What will you protect? What will you sacrifice your body for? Will you protect your brand? Your plate, the thing you have decided to protect, may be your family, your career, your community or your reputation. What are your priorities? It is part of the job description for a secret service agent to take a bullet for the President. What will you take a bullet for? Do you have what it takes to block the plate?

I developed a love for running when I was in law school. It was the first time I did not have organized sports in my life. I found it was a perfect antidote for the law school pressure cooker. I soon learned when you run a path you get to know the terrain like the palm of your hand. You know where the pavement dips, you know where the asphalt cracks and you know which homes have dogs. Some people have their dogs behind a fence. Others keep their dogs on a chain. There are some people who let their dogs run free.

I had a neighbor who let his German Shepherd run free. Whenever I would pass my neighbor's house the Shepherd would come charging off the porch. The Shepherd would chase me to the end of his property line.

There are Shepherds, and then there are "Strays." A Stray is easy to identify. A Stray is dirty, usually thin and without a collar. A Stray avoids eye contact.

In all my years of running, I have never been chased by a Stray. A Stray is not territorial. A Stray has nothing to protect. A Stray has no stake in the outcome. A Stray has no home plate to block.

Ethical leaders are Shepherds. Shepherds think globally. Shepherds continually ask what is in the best interest of the organization, not what is in their personal best interest. Strays live meal-to-meal. The goal of a Stray is survival. The goal of a Shepherd is leaving a legacy. A Stray merely shows up for work; a Shepherd looks for ways to improve the company.

Strays remain Strays by continually putting personal interest ahead of the interest of others, whether those "others" are the office, the company, the organization, or the family.

I remember when a group of Shepherds called "Leadership Detroit" came to visit the courthouse where I was a sitting judge. The group is composed of leaders in business, law, medicine and government. Members look outside of their fields and discuss strategies and solutions to society's most chronic problems. One of the members of the class asked me,

"What is the biggest problem facing a criminal court?" They wanted to know how to stem the tide of violence. I considered the lack of financial investment plaguing the inner city, but I concluded that the lack of personal investment hit the community far worse. The selfishness of those who have been blessed with education and wealth, which do not see themselves in the faces of those who may fall prey to the criminal justice system, is the problem. There are many people blessed with resources who do not think it is their responsibility to protect the plate of those less fortunate. We must stop dehumanizing certain segments of the community. We are in this together.

I was taught that none of us are anything until the least of us is something. The Association of Black Judges of Michigan established a mentoring program called "Each One, Reach One." If every able-bodied person made a commitment to reach one child, we could have a dramatic effect on curbing the crime rate.

Years ago I was coaching my son's little league baseball team. There was one parent who sat in his car during the games. When his son came up to bat, he got out of the car, moved up to the fence and cheered like crazy for his kid. After his son finished his turn at the plate, the dad walked back and got into his car. Amazingly, he would repeat this routine whenever his son came up to hit. This parent may have been a Shepherd to his son, but he was a Stray to the other players. He could not see how some of the other kids, some who did not have a parent at the game, could benefit from a cheer. He only cared about the game within the game. He could not see the selfishness he was teaching his son.

Sometimes selfishness is more subtle. I have been at sporting events where one parent is at the game. The other parent calls on the phone. The first word out of the mouth of the parent who is at the game is a detailed description of what their child has done during the game. The phone call may end with a statement of how the team is doing. The plight of the team is secondary to the plight of their kid. These self- absorbed parents have it backwards.

My daughter's high school basketball coach would encourage parents to call him to discuss any topic except for one. The off-limits topic was playing time. The coach drew a line in the sand. He recognized parents are too biased. They do not see the big picture. It was not a coincidence that the coach, Frank Orlando of Detroit Country Day, just happened to have the most wins in the history of Michigan high school girls' basketball.

Having a myopic view of the world does not make for ethical leaders. Ethical leaders must be able to see the big picture. Too often people focus only on how their behavior impacts them and not the organization. Ethical leaders must continually ask not what is in "my" best interest, but instead what is in the best interest of the organization. It becomes harder to recognize and appreciate the big picture when you have only heard cheers for you and not for the team.

I remember there was a player on my daughter's high school basketball team that had a serious leg injury and as a result could not play. Her dad still came to every home and away game and cheered for every basket as if his daughter was playing. He was the Shepherd protecting his daughter's team even though he had no official role. This dad was there at every game to lead the team in restoring the player's confidence when shots were missed, helping the team to bear the burdens of a loss and assisting the team in staying humble when they won.

I was in a mentoring program called "Man to Man" at Paul Robeson Academy in Detroit under the leadership of the school's principal, Ray Johnson. One of the mentors loved the game of chess. He volunteered to start a chess club. Through the game of chess, he taught life skills. He told the kids the key to being a good chess player is being able to think five moves ahead. There is also a consequence for every move you make.

The ability to think before you react is a valuable life lesson. The skill of being able to think ahead and strategically plan for the future is a valuable life lesson. The chess coach would always brag that none of his players ever got into trouble with the law. He credited the lessons learned from the game of chess as keeping them crime free. The coach would stress to the chess players that the choices they make now can shape the moves they would be able to make as adults.

The chess coach is a definite Shepherd. He made a conscious decision to block the plate. He protected our most sacred resource, our children. The chess master had a gift and decided to share it. Everyone has a gift. The question is: Will you share your gift? Will you use your gift or talent to protect the plate?

Every Sunday, when I want a newspaper, I go to the same newsstand. On this particular corner, for years there was a man who always has a team of teenage boys with him, selling papers. When I handed the boys the money for the paper, they always pleasantly say, "Thank you and have a nice day." Now that may not sound like much to you, but I am impressed when young people exhibit sincere respect to adults. Simply saying thank you has become a lost art in too many circles. I know the man who runs the corner has told them that customer service requires that deeply felt thank you. I predict that when the youngsters one day own their own companies, they will look back and be thankful for the Shepherd on the corner who taught them how to talk to customers.

We have the resources and technology to carry computers in our pockets, yet we are still scratching our heads trying to solve the crime problem. It is a question of commitment. We need Shepherds to step up. We need Shepherds in the business community. Business leaders should take pride in developing Shepherds—those who recognize that they have a stake in the company. Shepherds feel valued and appreciated. Shepherds take pride in the quality of their work. Strays will not go the extra mile to protect the company plate. Strays will do the bare bones minimum.

When leaders empower those that follow them through "buy-in", an ethical leader creates Shepherds out of Strays. Employees will only feel valued and contribute to the decision- making process if they know that the Shepherd recognizes that every single person at every level has value. The "buy-in" can be promoted by taking a genuine interest in the work/life balance of the workforce. Know what stage in life your employees are going through, and show genuine concern for their humanity, and you will help maximize their contribution to the bottom line. The employee that has to provide home health care to an elderly parent may need a more flexible work schedule. Recognizing the needs of employees is protecting the company's investment.

I learned that a simple act of kindness goes a long way. Simply saying "good job" or "I appreciate you working late" will not be forgotten. I was working on a case once with a young lawyer and she was amazed that I asked her, in a meeting with a client, "What do you think?" She said most partners simply gave her an assignment and do not ask her opinion, particularly in front of a client. I was not looking for her to be a potted plant. I welcomed her feedback. Ethical leaders look for ways to listen, affirm and validate the workforce.

I remember one day walking the halls of the United States Attorney's Office. There were more than two hundred employees spread out over multiple floors. Employees could go for months without seeing people on the other floors.

While I was walking one floor, I encountered an attorney who told me his son was sick.

Although we only talked for a short time, I never forgot the strain he was under performing this stressful job with a sick son at home. I tried to use what I learned about his situation whenever I had to make personnel decisions. My wife always says when she meets a person that she finds difficult, "You never know what people are going through." I now recognize that there are more dimensions to the people with whom I work. When I saw that attorney again, I asked him about his son. He told me his son was doing better. When I left the job, that attorney told me he never forgot me asking about his son. All of the cases and programs we worked on paled in comparison to the inquiry about his son. The fact that I took an interest in his personal life left an indelible impression.

You can also create buy-in by personally delivering "bad news." Case in point: selecting whom to promote among a number of candidates. An opportunity for a promotion in the U.S. Attorney's Office is an attractive proposition that would yield many prospects. It was easy to call the person who was chosen. But what about the other candidates? How do you tell them? Do you tell them by phone or e-mail? Do you delegate the task? Do you take no action and let the candidate find out on his/ her own?

I always made it a practice to tell the defeated candidates in person. Even though they were disappointed they did not get the promotion, they respected the fact that I took the time to come to their office and tell them face to face. I told them they were still a valued member of the team. Their morale was important for the continued success of the organization.

Shepherds are effective listeners. I am reminded of the doctor with a good bedside manner. The doctor does not rush the patient. The doctor is sensitive to the patient's vulnerable position. The doctor's ability to listen and not lecture makes the patient feel more comfortable.

I learned a lesson in how not to talk to people when my son was a freshman at the University of Michigan. One morning the phone rings at 2:30 a.m. The caller identification reads, "Ann Arbor Public Safety." My blood pressure shoots up. My chest is pounding. I answer the phone. The caller immediately identifies himself as an Ann Arbor Public Safety Officer. He then says, "Are you the father of Justin Collins?" My heart is now on the floor. You do not start a conversation at 2:30 in the morning with a question like this unless it is bad news. I fear the worst.

The officer explained that Justin left his wallet on a bus and the driver turned it in. The officer merely wanted me to contact Justin and tell him how he could get his wallet back. I wish he would have called me after sunrise or tried to start the conversation about his purpose for calling sooner. When you are in a position of authority, people cling to every word. Ethical leaders must be sensitive to how that word is conveyed.

Shepherds are also knowledgeable in publicly recognizing the talents of those whom they are shepherding. I learned this lesson on my daughter's first day of kindergarten. She was holding on to my wife's leg for dear life. However, during the leg strangulation, Jessica loosened her grip in order to tie her shoe. The teacher, Mrs. Stern, saw this and instantly announced to the entire class, "If anyone needs their shoes tied they are to see Jessica Collins immediately." Appreciating that her talent was welcomed and recognized, my daughter smiled at my wife and said, "See you at three o'clock." A Shepherd was being created.

Fast forward to Jessica's senior high school softball banquet. What an evening! She left with a wheelbarrow full of awards. Her coach said she was the best player he ever coached. She was recognized for being an All-State selection and the team MVP. Her career statistics were off the charts. However, the most impressive and insightful compliment came from a teammate. The teammate was not in awe of the awards. The teammate said that what she will remember most about Jessica is that she was her friend when no one else would be.

Now that is legacy.

There was a little league baseball coach named Ken Lewis. He coached for years in the Rosedale-Grandmont little league in Detroit. He gathered his team after every game. The outcome of the game did not matter. Coach Lewis would compliment every single player. He would tailor the compliment to every player. He would always find something positive to say about every player. He personalized the compliment. Even if a kid struck out four times and had two errors, Coach Lewis would find the positive: "You did not swing at any bad pitches," or "You gave it your best effort." Coach Lewis recognized the basic human desire to be affirmed and validated starts at an early age. The positive reinforcement created buy- in. He was creating Shepherds. We all should be determined to make "Shepherding" our lifelong brand.

Business leaders would learn a lot from Coach Lewis. Business leaders should be on the lookout and appreciate the good work of their employees. If a leader is oblivious to the good efforts of his team, it creates an atmosphere of complacency, as employees don't feel their efforts are recognized or valued.

If you consciously look for and celebrate the talents in others, you invariably leave a mark. One day I was watching a TV show about how people in a homeless shelter took up the game of soccer. It was a small but important step to rebuilding their defeated spirits. They received a tremendous amount of pride from playing soccer together. Many of those players, with their newly-found skill, ended up transitioning from a life of homelessness. They were encouraged. They learned to play on a team and take responsibility. They found ways to win, and strengthened their internal fortitude to combat the difficult position they were in.

I felt if the small step of being a part of a soccer team could have such a positive effect on people, then so could running. While I served on the Board of Directors of Neighborhood Service Organization (NSO), which offers a wide range of servicing programs that seeks to solve homelessness, I offered to start a fitness program.

To get the program off the ground I went to the homeless shelters serviced by NSO. I learned that a certain segment of the homeless population is working through substance abuse. At each shelter, I told the residents about my addiction to running. I challenged them to trade negative addiction for a positive addiction. I explained that our "recovery sessions" would meet every Saturday for twelve weeks at 7:00 a.m. at Cass Park in Detroit. I told them to expect to experience a runner's high.

Of course there were naysayers. There were some that said that they couldn't run. Many thought the program would not work. Critics were quick to point out that I was dealing with a transient population and it was unlikely anyone would consistently show up. I ignored the negative feedback and marched onward. The program was a huge success.

On the first day I arrived at 6:45 a.m. There was a lady, Ms. Epps, who was sitting on a park bench. She proudly boasted, "I'm here first." I told her, "From now on, your nickname is No. 1." By 7:00 a.m. there were twenty participants. We stretched, did some jumping jacks and push-ups, and we jogged around the park. Some walked, some ran and some did a little of both. At the end of the workout there were bagels and juice.

For twelve weeks in a row, no one could beat Ms. Epps' arriving first, even despite my persistent challenges. Due to her preexisting health limitation, she could not participate in all of the exercises, but every week we celebrated the fact that she was always there first. At the end of the twelve weeks, I gave her a medal that said "No. 1." You would have thought she had won an Olympic gold medal; she was bursting with pride. Acknowledging what she did well kept her coming back every week. She had carved out a stake in the fitness program. Positive reinforcement works in all walks of life.

Finally, ethical leaders create Shepherds by admitting their mistakes. We live in a very forgiving society. We are a country that prides itself on giving people a second chance. Too often people compound the problem and dig a deeper hole by not admitting the mistake. The bleeding does not stop, it gets worse. Sometimes the cover-up is bigger than the crime. Ironically, it takes ethics to admit an ethical mistake. People respect leaders that take responsibility.

In all of my years doing white-collar criminal defense work, I have found only rarely will a client, in the initial meeting, admit the mistake. Only once did I have a client who told me in the very first consultation that everything in the indictment was true. I was shocked. There was no blame shifting. There was no minimization. There were no denials. There was no dragging it out of him. It did not take months and months of "Come to Jesus" meetings in order for him to take ownership of the mistake.

I remember the State of Wayne County speech of 2012. At the time of the speech the County was under siege. We were still reeling from the mistakes of the past. It was critical for the CEO to admit that mistakes were made under his watch. It was important for him to be specific, and to identify and take ownership of the mistakes. It was most important for him to be sincere about his responsibility for the problem. You cannot have a recovery until you sincerely acknowledge the illness. Admitting that you are responsible for the mistake is a defining moment in regaining credibility as an ethical leader. Trying to defend unethical behavior only makes matters worse. As it turned out, the CEO publicly admitted that mistakes were made. He acknowledged that he made a mistake by not keeping a close watch on his staff. This admission was the most well received part of the speech.

Arrogance is the graveyard for ethical leadership. Ethics requires humility. When the Department of Justice was investigating whether the Detroit Police Department was violating the civil rights of citizens, I met with City of Detroit officials. The investigation focused on whether conditions of confinement for prisoners were humane, whether the police department was using excessive force during arrests, and whether witnesses were being unlawfully detained in order to extract statements. In my initial meeting with city officials they said, "There is nothing you can tell us that we don't already know." I found this statement troubling. One of the city officials had only been on the job a few months. How could he possibly know all of the problems of the police department? It was like a parent saying, "There is nothing you can tell me about my teenage child that I don't already know." As a parent, if you think you know all of the things your child is doing, you are only fooling yourself. Did your parent know all the things you were doing?

The findings of the investigation turned out to be very severe. That is why I recommended a Consent Decree and not a Memorandum of Understanding. The Consent Decree provided the toughest mechanism for enforcement and oversight.

The failure of city officials to admit there could be things the police department did not know about was a fundamental lack of humility. No one knows it all. No one has all of the answers. It takes humility to say, "I don't know." It takes humility to say, "I need help." It takes humility to accept responsibility.

Admitting your vulnerability shows strength, not weakness.

The full story of what was going on in the police department could only be discovered after a complete and thorough investigation. The most significant progress in implementing many of the recommended changes occurred only after a new mayor, Dave Bing, was elected and a new city administration was installed. The new administration acknowledged the problem and made addressing it a priority. Strays will remain Strays if the tone at the top is dominated by arrogance. Arrogance does not seek a second opinion. Arrogance does not seek buy-in. Arrogance does not respect other points of view. Arrogance places a chokehold on the free flow of ideas. Arrogance does not like others to challenge their views. It is difficult for an ethical voice to gain traction or to flourish in an environment that feeds on arrogance.

When I was a judge on the Michigan Court of Appeals, I often formed a preliminary opinion about the case, from the briefs the lawyers would file with the court. In addition, the Michigan Court of Appeals had excellent staff attorneys who would "brief the briefs." They would provide the judges with a summary of each side of the case as well as a proposed decision. While these tools were extremely helpful, I would never say, after reviewing these briefs as well as the "briefs of the briefs," that "I know it all." At oral argument, a lawyer could raise a point you had not considered. At oral argument, a lawyer could analyze an issue in a manner that would impact or change the way you were leaning.

After oral argument, the judges would caucus. Unlike the trial court where the judge sits alone, cases are heard by three-judge panels in the Michigan Court of Appeals. Another judge during the caucus could raise a point that impacts or changes the other judges' thinking. The process is designed to be inclusive, so it was important to keep an open mind. Input from staff, law clerks and other judges all help in arriving at the right decision. It would be foolish to start the process with the declaration, "There is nothing you can tell me I don't already know."

It is important if you are blessed to be in a position of power to have the courage to speak the truth. Shepherds speak the truth. Shepherds speak the truth under the glare of the public spotlight and when no one is watching. I was presented with both of these extremes when, as the new United States Attorney, in 2001 I inherited a public corruption investigation into Wayne County government.

The investigation advanced to a point where probable cause existed that a crime was committed and evidence of the commission of that crime was in the Wayne County offices. The election for Governor occurred at the time we were prepared to ask a federal judge to sign a search warrant allowing the raid. The ethical question became one of timing. Do we seek judicial approval before or after the election? The Democratic candidate for governor was the former chief attorney of the administration under investigation. The Republican candidate was the Lt. Governor whose administration supported my nomination to be United States Attorney.

The Cynic would expect I would seek approval and execution of the search warrant before the election. The Cynic would presume I would do an official act that could benefit the political party that put me in office. The Slickster would take it one step further and even time the raid to occur on the eve of the election. This would give the Democratic candidate less time to respond.

I did not take the route of either the Cynic or the Slickster. I waited a few weeks after the election to seek judicial approval of the warrant. As it turned out, the Democratic candidate won a very close election. A highly publicized raid may have changed the outcome. I did not believe the integrity of the investigation would suffer by waiting until after the election. There was absolutely no evidence that the Democratic candidate had done anything wrong. The brand of the Department of Justice is not to be guided by politics. Investigations are driven by the evidence and should not be politically motivated. By waiting until after the election to execute the search warrant, the Department of Justice connected ethics to action. This was done very quietly, but very effectively.

Once the raid occurred, another ethical issue arose. There were a number of public officials associated with Wayne County government that were not the targets of the investigation. The ethical issue was whether I should issue a public statement saying they were not suspects.

Issuing exonerating statements is not a part of the brand

of the Department Justice. Issuing statements like this had never been done before in the history of the Detroit United States Attorneys' office and to my knowledge had rarely if ever been done by other United States Attorneys' offices in the country. I felt the mere fact it had not been done before did not mean it should not be done. I could not let the absence of precedent interfere with doing the right thing. Even though it was not the practice, custom or policy of the Department of Justice to issue such statements did not mean it was not the right thing to do. The facts were clear. These public officials were not suspected of wrongdoing. This was the simple truth. I felt it was important to speak the truth.

Cynics would warn against making such statements. Cynics would argue that it was too early in the investigation to make any statements. Cynics would advocate waiting until all of the evidence seized from the raid is reviewed and analyzed before issuing a public statement. However, the process of reviewing all of the evidence could take many months and even years to complete. In the meantime, these public officials would be operating under a cloud of suspicion. They had offices to run where their credibility was on the line. The public statements removed the cloud. Issuing the statements and clearing the air was the right thing to do.

PRACTICE TIP

You can become a "Shepherd" by:

1. Identifying and publicly recognizing the talents of people around you
2. Embracing the power of encouragement
3. Speaking the truth
4. Taking ownership of mistakes
5. Firing arrogance and hiring humility

CHAPTER FIVE

Caught In A Pickle

A baseball rundown, often called a "pickle", is when you have a base runner trapped between two bases. Fielders are on both sides of the runner throwing the ball back and forth trying to tag the runner out. Caught between two bases, the runner is in a pickle. Ethically, you can get caught in a pickle, too, trapped between two decisions that have important ethical implications. Sometimes, they can change the trajectory of your life.

I was presented with an ethical dilemma a few years ago. I was a partner at Law Firm #1 and received an offer to work for Law Firm #2. I decided to accept the offer from Law Firm #2. I was scheduled to receive a substantial bonus from Law Firm #1.

The job with Law Firm #2 was scheduled to start after I received the bonus from Law Firm #1. Do I tell Law Firm #1 about the job I accepted with Law Firm #2? I feared if I told Law Firm #1, they would not pay me the bonus. To tell or not to tell created an ethical dilemma. I was caught in a rundown.
In deciding what to do, I ran the dilemma through an ethical filter test.

Question #1: *Does it violate the law?* If so, end of discussion and you tell Law Firm #1 about the job. If no law is being broken by not telling Law Firm #1, you proceed to the second ethical filter question.

Question #2: *Does it violate a policy?* In my situation there was no company policy or internal rules that addressed the issue. Thus far, I appeared to be on safe ground in not disclosing the new job. However, there were more ethical boxes to check.

Question#3: *How would it look on the front page of a newspaper?* Appearances count. Lawyers are taught to avoid even the appearance of impropriety. Even if it does not violate a law or a policy, if it looks bad, we should avoid it. For example, it looks bad for a vendor to give lavish gifts to family members of a public servant even if there are no rules that prohibit it.

In my dilemma, I felt there was not an appearance problem. The bonus was for past performance. I had earned it. In my mind the new job and the bonus from the old job were separate and distinct issues. I would feel comfortable if my story was broadcast on the evening news. Therefore, I had to go to the fourth and final filter question, the last line of your ethical defense.

Question #4: *Does it violate your personal code?* Question #4 forces you to prioritize values. Question #3 invites the question,

"Would it be ok if everyone did it?" Question #4 digs deeper by asking, "Even if everyone else is doing it, is it the right thing to do?" In this case, I asked how much did I value leaving Job #1 on good terms. I used a cost-benefit analysis. I weighed the importance of short- term financial gain against the long-term gain of having a reputation no one will question. If the shoe were on the other foot, wouldn't I want to know? This was a flashback to the question my mom asked me in the store after the candy bar theft, namely, how I would feel if I were the owner of the store. The bottom line was could I look myself in the mirror if I did not tell?

I am proud to say I told Law Firm #1 of the new job before the bonus was due. By telling Law Firm #1 of the new job, I was voluntarily relinquishing control of the outcome. I had to be prepared to lose the bonus. There was no guarantee Law Firm #1 would pay the bonus. Ethical leadership has a price. The possibility of losing the substantial bonus was the price I might have to pay to claim ethical victory.

The ball was now in their court. The burden shifted to Law Firm #1; they would now have to run through the same ethical filter test. They had to ask themselves whether not paying the bonus violated any laws or company policies. They had to ask whether there was an appearance problem with not paying a former employee a bonus. They had to ask themselves about their own personal ethical code as the organization. Could the organization look itself in the mirror if it refused to pay the bonus?

The law firm could rationalize nonpayment by saying, "Why pay the bonus to someone who is leaving?" They could argue that one of the purposes of the bonus is to encourage future loyalty to the organization. By paying the bonus they would not receive a benefit for their investment in the future of the organization. Finally, the company may deny paying the bonus for an irrational reason, simply out of spite or anger. The ethical core of the firm would be revealed.

I am happy to say Law Firm #1 did the right thing. They paid the bonus without hesitation. Because I left on good terms, Law Firm #1 would later refer me cases and be very supportive of my career. Likewise, I have always spoken highly of the firm. Their reputation as an ethical firm was reinforced through my experience. The decision to tell them of the new job resulted in a win-win.

At the Department of Justice in my role as U.S. Attorney, I found myself in another pickle. This one was during the nation's first terrorism trial, which occurred after the horrific events of 9/11 and was conducted by attorneys that I supervised. Let me preface this story by stating emphatically:

The mission of the Department of Justice is not to obtain convictions, but to secure justice.

Ethical leaders must understand their priorities before they can implement them. Once you perceive what is most important, and for the Department of Justice it is "securing justice", then you have taken an important step toward getting out of the pickle.

The terrorism trial tested our priorities. With the Department of Justice, the goal of winning takes a back seat to winning the right way. The role of the federal prosecutor is to strike hard blows, not foul ones. The ethical question becomes, "Where do you draw the line?" What is a hard blow and what is a foul blow? When the prosecutor straddles the line, he or she finds themselves in a pickle.

I was in Washington, D.C. attending a meeting with the Attorney General's Advisory Committee at the Department of Justice (DOJ), also called "Main Justice" by the local DOJ offices. The Committee is made up of United States Attorneys from across the country. They discussed national law enforcement priorities and initiatives with the Attorney General of the United States. Suddenly, I was called out of the meeting.

High-ranking officials in the Justice Department were conducting a conference call with the prosecutors on the case from our Detroit office. They wanted me to join them on the call. The Department of Justice officials had a ton of questions. The lead prosecutor answered each and every question with poise and precision. I believed that the lead attorney had a complete mastery of the facts. At the next staff meeting in Detroit, I even recognized and complimented him on how he conducted himself during the call.

Despite the impressive presentation made by the lead attorney in the conference call however, tensions were growing between our office and the officials in Washington. What initially felt like a turf war over trial strategy was turning into teammates now suspicious of each other. The lead prosecutor's exemplary handling of the conference call was in stark contrast to his conduct in another meeting when Main Justice officials visited my office in Detroit. At this meeting, a justice official asked the lead prosecutor the basis for a theory in the indictment. The lead prosecutor said he got the theory from an appellate lawyer in our office. The Washington justice official asked where the appellate lawyer got the theory. The lead prosecutor rudely replied, "What do you think, he blew it out of his ass?"

Roadblocks to transparency raise red flags. Not wanting anyone to know or to challenge how you come up with a decision does not promote confidence in the decision. Ethical leaders have no problem having their decisions reviewed, debated and criticized. Ethical leaders want the focus to remain on prioritized principles. They encourage checks on compliance with ethical principles without feeling a personal attack on their integrity. Even though we were on the same team fighting for the same goal, the lead prosecutor resisted sharing information with his teammates. As this was the first terrorism trial post 9/11 in the country, Main Justice was keeping a close eye on the case. Combating terrorism was the top law enforcement priority of the country. The frequent complaints about the flow of information to Main Justice foreshadowed a larger problem that would lead to the dismissal of the case.

To solve the communication problem, the Deputy Attorney General of the United States sent a Department of Justice lawyer to our Detroit office. He was to be a valued member of the trial team. He was instructed to sit in the courtroom during each day of the trial. It was felt this would insure timely and complete information for the officials in Washington.

As it turned out, the Department of Justice lawyer was excluded from the trial team. He was not included in all of the case strategy meetings. Later, he explained that he believed if he complained, then the treatment would only worsen. Therefore, he did not share his complaints with his superiors during the trial.

Despite the tensions, we were able to obtain guilty convictions on key counts in the indictment. Following the verdicts, questions were raised about the fairness of the prosecution. The defendants complained they were not provided all of the relevant information held by the government. Understand that the prosecution is required, by law, to provide all information, whether favorable or unfavorable, to the defense. Even information that could possibly lead to an acquittal must be shared.

When I believed that fundamental rules of sharing information had been violated, I made the decision to remove the lead prosecutor from the case. In my opinion, ethical leadership required this.

Following the removal, the Department of Justice asked the court to throw out the convictions. The government conceded that it did not play by the rules. By not sharing all of information with the defendants, the verdict was contaminated. The defendants did not receive a fair trial because they were not provided all of the information to assist in their defense. The possibility of someone going to prison based on a contaminated verdict is unconstitutional, unconscionable and antithetical to our commitment to justice and to our nation's laws.

By asking the court to toss out the case after obtaining convictions, the Department of Justice showed that it was prepared to pay the cost of ethical leadership. The Department of Justice was prepared to sacrifice all of the hours and resources invested in the case to support the overarching mission of securing justice. The Department of Justice was prepared to lose the case if it meant furthering the greater good. The Department of Justice was prepared to take the public scolding and embarrassment of mishandling a high profile case concerning its top law enforcement priority. The national significance of the case did not make the Department of Justice shrink from its responsibility to do the right thing. While many may say this terrorism trial was one of the failures of the Department of Justice, in the final analysis, by doing the right thing, the trial was really one of its finest moments. It is one instance of America fulfilling its promise of justice for all.

Many people think that doing criminal defense work would create an ethical pickle. The question defense attorney's get all the time is, "How can you represent someone if you know they are guilty?" People want to know if this creates an ethical dilemma. The answer is, simply, "No." The Constitution provides everyone with the right to counsel. The Constitution does neither distinguish between the types of cases nor the types of people that should be afforded representation. The defense attorney's loyalty is to the U.S. Constitution.

To execute that loyalty means the criminal defense attorney must aggressively hold the government to its burden of proof. The defense attorney understands his constitutional duty is not to judge, but to defend. For the defense attorney to maintain her loyalty and enthusiasm to the Constitution despite challenging or distasteful facts takes ethical strength. Critics of defense attorneys seem to have a greater appreciation for the presumption of innocence and proof beyond a reasonable doubt if they or a family member are ever charged with a crime. By doing their job, the defense attorney protects the freedom of all of us.

I consider the trial arena as a three-legged stool. The judge, the prosecutor and the defense attorney each make up a leg of the stool. Each plays a key role in upholding justice. If any leg is out of place, the entire stool can collapse. Our judicial system works magnificently when all of the players uphold their end of the deal.

Early in my law practice, I represented the leader of a notorious drug organization. The organization was entitled "Young

Boys Inc." (YBI) and its leader was Butch Jones.

I represented Butch Jones in three murder cases. During jury selection, the Honorable George Crockett, III, asked one juror to look at another juror. He asked the first juror if the second juror looked guilty. The first juror said "no." Judge Crockett than asked the first juror to look around the entire courtroom and tell him if anyone in the courtroom looked guilty. Again, the juror said "no." The judge concluded the line of questioning by asking the juror did she know of anyone that had the power to look at someone and tell they are guilty. Again the answer was "no."

This line of questioning was designed to rebut the common view that sitting in the defendant's chair means you must have done something wrong. Butch Jones received a fair trial because jurors did not allow prejudgments to impact the decision.

I have found whether I was representing Butch Jones or prosecuting a case or presiding over a case that "honesty" is the key. Do not make promises you cannot keep. Do not create false hopes. Keep your word. Give the case your very best effort. Be passionate in your position. And by all means treat everybody with respect and dignity. Armed with these basic fundamentals, I had a way to resolve the ethical dilemmas that confronted me.

Trial attorneys are trained not to ask questions for which they do not know the answer. This is a fundamental rule of cross- examination. The danger is the witness may say something the trial attorney does not want to hear. In the heat of battle it takes discipline and restraint not to venture into uncharted waters.

Likewise, the ethical leader must stick to his ethical code. Ethical leaders get in trouble when they veer from their code. In the heat of making an ethical decision, you must stay true to your personal ethical code.

More Pickles, More Problems

When the person you report to exhibits unethical conduct, you find yourself in a pickle. You may have worked with the wrongdoer for years and developed a friendship. You may see other redeeming qualities in this person, but now he wants you to look the other way. You may serve at the pleasure of the superior and he sets your compensation. There is no doubt in your mind that he has chosen the wrong course for the company. What do you do?

First, look for another point of access. Who does the "on-paper" decision maker listen to? That is really the one making the decision. That is where the real power lies in an organization. Who has the decision maker's ear? Identify that person and seek their support in bringing truth to power. You may be barking up the wrong tree if you fail to identify the real decision maker.

Secondly, identify an influential group that supports your position and take that group to the decision maker. You need to rally the people who share your views. There is strength in numbers. Consider the "management team" approach as an intervention. The decision maker needs to know the complaint is not simply your complaint, but that many share the same concern. If the problem is viewed as isolated or unique to you, the person in charge can easily dismiss it.

As a judge I often would hear young defendants say they committed a crime because they were hanging with the wrong crowd. The very same thing is true in the corporate culture. Too

often the corporate culture is a lot like the culture of the young defendant on trial for what might be considered "street criminal" behavior: A corporate team member can similarly be influenced to engage in unethical, even criminal behavior because of their corporate "peers." Too often people surround themselves with others who think like them. Instead, they should surround themselves with those who think like themselves.
Thirdly, determine what motivates the decision maker. Is he a big picture thinker?

Before you change his mind, you may need to encourage a different way of thinking through the decision. How does the manager think through an ethical issue?

There are countless approaches to resolving ethical issues. There is the **Common Good Approach**. This approach looks to make decisions that best serve the community as a whole, not just some members. The Little League parent that only watches and cheers his kid and not the team as a whole violates the Common Good Approach.

There is also the **Justice Approach** which mandates that all people be treated equally. Allowing select employees to come in late, take long lunches and leave early violates the Justice Approach. These models appeal to a sense of fairness.

The decision maker could adopt a solution that causes the Least Harm. This is also known as the utilitarian approach to resolving ethical issues. This approach looks to maximize pleasure and minimize pain. It favors an outcome that benefits the greatest good for the greatest number. In my view, the **Least Harm Approach** may clash with the right thing to do. Even if the decision hurts only a few, if it is the right thing to do, the ethical leader does it. The "Least Harm" approach may give the decision maker an easy way out and the opportunity to avoid making the tough decision.

The model that we should be adopting is the **Virtue Approach.** The Virtue Approach is aspirational. It is what we should be striving for. It sets a high standard. Aspirational leadership is reflected in the work of the Honorable Gershwin Drain, who currently serves as U.S. District Court for the Eastern District of Michigan.

One day I received a phone call from Judge Drain who was then a sitting judge on the Detroit Recorder's Court bench. He asked me to be a guest speaker at a worship service. I assumed the invitation was to his church. However, to my surprise, he gave me the address of Ryan Correctional Facility, a prison in northeast Detroit.

I came to learn that every month Judge Drain went to Ryan Correctional Facility and conducted a full-scale worship service. There was song, praise and prayer. Judge Drain or a guest would also deliver a message. Prisoners explained that their families did not regularly visit them, but Judge Drain was there consistently every month. It would not be uncommon for Judge Drain to be holding hands in prayer with a prisoner that he previously sentenced to imprisonment.

I was impressed by Judge Drain's humility. To volunteer to lead a prison ministry is aspirational leadership at its very best. Our daily walk should include helping the least of these. A true sign of ethical leadership is how you treat people who cannot do anything for you in return.

The Virtue Approach recognizes that we are all equipped to do extraordinary things. The Virtue Approach pushes us to go beyond what is expected. The goal is to incorporate the extraordinary into our personal ethical code. The Virtue Approach recognizes that caring is the engine that powers ethics.

I remember traveling home after watching the U.S. Open tennis tournament. My court officer, Eric "Gio" Giovannini, was driving. We were stopped on the Ohio Turnpike. The State Trooper approached the vehicle and asked Gio what took him so long to pull over. The trooper explained that he had been following us for miles. Gio said it was a narrow highway and he did not want to pull over until there was enough room that would allow the trooper to get out of his vehicle safely. The trooper said, "You cared about me, no one ever cares about me." The trooper turned around and said, "you guys have a nice day." No ticket because Gio actually cared about the well being of someone else.

Companies are becoming increasingly sensitive to the importance of genuinely caring about the welfare of its employees. Providing employees with extended medical leave to deal with a serious illness will make the employee more loyal than ever. I believe a caring ethical model makes for a stronger bottom line. Morale and staff retention is high in this environment. A happy employee is a productive employee. Efficiency is improved. Employees and clients are attracted to organizations that genuinely care about their well being.

Starbucks is a great example of the Virtue Approach. They offer their workers free college tuition. Employees do not have to repay Starbucks nor do they have to stay on with the company. Starbucks believes that investing in its employees is the right thing to do. They place a priority on students being able to graduate debt free. The cost Starbucks will incur in paying tuition is outweighed by the commitment to allow workers to pursue their dreams unencumbered with debt. What a brand!

Opposite the Justice Approach, Common Good Approach and the Virtue Approach is the **Self-Interest Approach**. The decision maker may not be swayed by what is in the best interest of the organization. Instead, he may be swayed by what is in his personal best interest. This is known as an ethical egoist. For the ethical egoist, the right thing to do is governed by self-interest. The ethical egoist feels no obligation to help or care for others. The ethical egoist does not ask, "What is in it for us?" Instead, the ethical egoist asks, "What is in it for me?" If the decision maker is selfish, speak to him in a language that he understands. The number one rule in sales is to show the buyer how the sale benefits him.

One important thing to remember: Never ambush the person in charge with your complaint. Give them time to prepare a thoughtful response. Try to avoid publicly embarrassing the person. Try to devise a solution that allows the decision maker to save face.

Despite your diplomacy, tempers may still flare when you confront the decision maker over an unethical decision. Remember, the hit dog screams the loudest. Ignore the drama. Remain focused on the facts. You do not want your complaint to get lost in a shouting match. Do not condemn the decision maker, condemn the facts. Do not personalize the complaint. People tend to harden their positions and become even more entrenched when the argument becomes personal.

You should be commended for having the courage to report misconduct. As a kid, being a "tattletale" is considered bad.

In street culture, being a "snitch" is frowned upon. But when it comes to corporate America, or public sector jobs, laws and rules have been established to protect whistleblowers. A "code of silence" is widely observed in a wide variety of work and social settings and it takes courage to break the code. Behind the scenes, employees often complain about the work culture. However they suddenly go mute when they are presented with the chance to complain directly to the decision maker. People feel intimidated to speak truth to power.

People can easily become financial hostages to an unethical work environment. The benefits of being ethical are often weighed against the financial realities of being without a job. Only you can decide what is nonnegotiable. Do not draw a line in the sand only to erase it to draw another one. The slippery slope can be very dangerous. People can compromise their ethics to the point where there is no line at all.

Run the issue through the ethical filter test. If the answer to any of the four questions (Law violation? Policy Violation? Bad front page? Personal ethics?) is "Yes," then leaving becomes the only option. You do not want your failure to leave to be viewed as a tacit approval of the improper conduct. It is important to document the disagreement and the steps taken to deter the conduct.

Paying the Price

There is a price to pay to be an ethical leader. You have to be prepared to take the "L". A high school student told me, instead of committing plagiarism she would rather take the "L." She would rather take the "loss" of a bad grade than compromise her ethics. Likewise, the ethical athlete would rather lose the game playing fair than to win by playing unfair. To claim the ethical victory may mean losing the game on the field. The ethical leader takes no pride in winning the battle and losing the ethical war. Taking the "L" may mean losing a case, losing a bonus or losing your job.

What if you are coaching third base and the runner misses the bag. You clearly see the runner's foot does not touch the bag and he goes on to score a run. What do you do? Do you tell the umpire? Would the answer change if it was the winning run in the championship game? What if the game was a rout? For the ethical leader the answer is not "it depends." The ethical leader's answer is the same regardless of the situation. Just as there is no such thing as being a little bit pregnant there is no such thing as being a little bit ethical. The ethical third base coach has to be prepared to lose the game in order to claim the ethical victory.

Companies, like the third base coach, can face an ethical dilemma when they discover unethical conduct. The question is do they self-report? Do they alert the authorities of the violation? Many companies struggle with this question because they fear the consequences. The easy thing to do is sweep it under the rug. However, the right thing to do is rarely the easy thing to do. The company has to be prepared to take the "L." Self-reporting may result in a financial loss or a loss in reputation. It could also mean someone losing their freedom. It could also mean some bad press. Ironically, the Department of Justice had rewarded companies that self-reported unlawful behavior. It is a mitigating factor that is taken into account in determining the disposition of the case. For a company to put bad conduct on the radar of a law enforcement agency that has the power to impose sanctions will be a true test of the company's ethical brand.

Seasoned trial attorneys know the benefit of volunteering bad news to the jury. It is better if the jury hears about the weaknesses in your case from you first, rather than from your opponent. Not only does it desensitize the jury to the unfavorable evidence, the credibility of the volunteering attorney rises. There are benefits to having the ethical courage to volunteer damaging evidence.

PRACTICE TIP

Identify the traps that have the potential to compromise your ethical code. Common traps include greed for money, power or fame. Boldly declare the ethical line you won't cross.

CHAPTER SIX

What Is Your Morning Glory?

I have always been a morning person. As a student, my most productive study hours came early in the morning. Late at night the law of diminishing returns would kick in and I would get a fresh start in the morning. My granddad was a morning person, too. He was a sharecropper in Virginia. He would always awaken before dawn and tend to his crops. He found peace in farming. Even during his last illness, the farm provided solace and contentment early in the morning.

I have found glory in running early in the morning. I find peace on the quiet pavements. I find glory in giving it my best.

I find glory in getting the heart pounding and the legs turning. Even if the night before you wonder how will I get the strength to run in the morning, somehow it comes. In the spring, seeing the beauty of the trees from opposite sides of the street meeting in the middle to form a forest tunnel, gives me so much inspiration.

I remember one wintry Friday morning run. It was a morning that tested your commitment to 5:00 a.m. running. The wind chill was well below zero and the high temperature was a single digit. Thoughts of rolling over in the bed instead of facing the freakishly cold wind churn through your head. Peer pressure has its value. But for the running group, I probably would have opted to stay in bed.

On Fridays, we end our run across the street from a bus stop. On this particular bitter cold Friday, I saw a man in a wheelchair trying to get on the bus. People were lifting the wheelchair onto the bus ramp. I looked at that and felt how blessed I was to be able to run. Even though the running conditions were miserable, I was physically able to put one foot in front of the other. Not everyone has that ability. I am sure if you asked the man in the wheelchair, he would also have a testimony about his joy in being able to ride the bus. There are things in his life to be thankful for. The fact that you have life is a blessing. The fact that you can always be an inspiration to others is a blessing. The fact that you are able to wake up and feel the crisp air of winter is a blessing.

Maybe that's why the "morning glory" flower has always intrigued me. It unravels into full bloom in the early morning and then wilts in the afternoon and dies. A new flower will bloom each morning. Each flower has just one day to display its glory before another flower comes to take its place.

Likewise, our lives are not guaranteed. We have to celebrate every day and be grateful for it. We have to find glory in each and every moment.

In baseball and life, you want to have a quality at bat. You want to make every bat count. You may not get a single, a double or a triple but it can still be a quality at bat. You may foul off ten pitches before you strike out, but you make the pitcher work so hard the next batter hits a home run. All the box score will show is that you got out. It will not show how you battled or that you added value to the team that day. Every day you want to strive to have a quality at bat.

At Wayne County, every day I pushed for greater transparency and more accountability. I tried to change the conversation. Ethical awareness has been enhanced. The commitment to change the culture may not show up in the box score, but ethical leaders cannot get discouraged. Ethical leaders cannot let the absence of credit prevent them from doing the right thing. Credit and recognition may not come from doing the right thing. You may not get a pat on the back. For me, doing the right thing brings an internal peace like my grandfather felt tending to his crops. The reward is intrinsic.

Every time you get a chance to hit, you want to strive to have a quality at bat. The greatest compliment I ever received as a judge came from an elderly women. She told me she had never been to downtown Detroit in her entire life. She went on to say she had never been to court her entire life. Even though she had no connection to the court system she told me, "I feel better knowing you are here." I took that ammunition with me to work every day. I wanted to have a quality day for the people who placed confidence in the decisions I would make.

Every single day you should strive to do your very best. You want to give it your best in school and on your job. You want to be the best person you can by giving something back to the community.

One of the former captains of my daughter's high school softball team was tragically killed in a car accident as she drove home for Thanksgiving vacation during her freshman year in college. Her driving saved the lives of the other passengers in the car. She died at 18 years of age. The box score will read she lived 18 years. The box score will not capture the quality of those 18 years. At a candle light vigil, there was an outpouring of emotion. Julie Karmann touched so many lives in sports, in theatre, and in school. Friends, teammates, classmates, teachers, and family all spoke on how Julie impacted them. The overriding message was that Julie lived life to the fullest. She had a quality life at bat. She found her morning glory in softball, theater, family and friends. She shared her glory with all who met her.

My administrative assistant, Renee Redding, died at the age of 36. On the day she died, I was hosting a community rally at Wayne State University entitled, "Off the Hook, Calling all Mentors." The purpose of the rally was to raise the awareness of the need for mentors and to allow mentoring programs from across the state an opportunity to sign up more volunteers. Renee was the glue in helping to organize the rally.

During the rally Renee, out of nowhere, collapsed. She was rushed to the hospital. We waited at the hospital hoping for good news. We were able to visit with her and she appeared to be improving. Later that day, Renee suffered an aneurysm and died instantly.

At the funeral, the family asked if anyone wanted to make a statement. It seemed as if the entire audience stood up. The line was wrapped around the room. Everyone who spoke had a similar story to tell. They said what a great friend Renee was and how her kindness touched their lives. One lady said Renee helped her plan her wedding. Another friend said how Renee was her support during a divorce. Another person said Renee helped him get a job. Another person said Renee did volunteer work for his campaign. On the day she died, she was helping me at the rally. She didn't have to come; it wasn't required for her job. The length of the line and the heartfelt testimonies were the best possible eulogy. Renee found her morning glory in helping others.

John Maxwell, an internationally recognized leadership expert and author, credits Walt Disney for describing three kinds of people in the world. There are "well-poisoners," who discourage you and tell you what you can't do. There are "lawn-mowers," people who are well intentioned, but self-absorbed; they mow their own lawns and never leave their yards to help another person. Finally, there are "life- enhancers," people who reach out to enrich the lives of others, to lift them up and inspire them.

Julie and Renee were life-enhancers. Ethical leaders are life-enhancers. You are blessed if you were raised in a village of life-enhancers. Parents, coaches, educators, religious leaders, neighbors, co-workers and friends have all at different points in my life served as life -enhancers. It is empowering to surround yourself with life- enhancers. Just as a runner draws energy from the person running next to him shoulder to shoulder, the ethical leader draws inspiration from the unselfishness of life-enhancers.

Renee's life motivates me to continually ask, "What am I doing to improve the lives of others?"

I learned through my nephew, Eric Miller, that many families in Chicago who could not afford to buy Christmas gifts for their children would write letters to Santa asking for gifts. The letters were collected at the post office. Each letter contained the name and ages of the kids and a gift wish list. Thanks to Eric, our family has made it a tradition to pick up letters from the post office to answer wishes. I have watched my wife buy gifts for complete strangers before she buys gifts for our kids. We buy, wrap and deliver the gifts.

One year, we pulled up to a house that was completely dark. We knocked on the door and there was no answer. I thought the house was abandoned or that we had a bad address. While my family was walking back to the car, a kid in a T-shirt without shoes on came running out of the house on this cold Chicago winter evening. "Don't go!" he yelled. As we were unloading the gifts from the car for the shoeless boy and his brothers, we learned that his mother was at work. We also learned the house was dark because they had no electricity and likely no heat. Although it was my plan to be the Christmas angel that day, the boy gave my family a lesson we will never forget.

My children learned to appreciate having a warm and well-lit house. My wife and I learned to appreciate not having to leave our children home alone while we worked. I learned to appreciate the opportunity to make a little difference in the life of another family. This is a taste of "morning glory." In retrospect, I wish I had done more. I wish I had gone back to the family to offer help in getting the lights back on. Don't I have an ethical duty to take action?

What is your morning glory? What inspires you to be a better person? On airplanes, the flight attendant always says if there is trouble and the oxygen mask comes down, be sure to put the mask on yourself before you put it on others. This sounds counter-intuitive, particularly for a parent who will instinctively want to protect their child first. The reason for the rule is that you cannot be of any help to your neighbor until you have yourself together. Finding your morning glory is like putting on that oxygen mask.

Your morning glory gives you the strength to face the day. It gives you the courage, the stamina and the tenacity to fight the naysayers. It gives you the fortitude to stand strong in the midst of a storm. It keeps you uplifted when the pace of change becomes frustrating. The ethical leader gains strength from his or her morning glory. Morning glory is the source of your strength. It is where you find inspiration. Morning glory encourages you to get the most out of every day. There is no time to waste.

Your morning glory helps to define your personal code. It is part of your brand. When there is a line you should not cross, morning glory will keep you on the right side of the line. Your morning glory may be preparing breakfast for your children. Your morning glory may be the smell of pancakes as you wake up. It may be saying a few words to God in prayer. It may be working in the garden. It may be keeping a journal—writing this book has been therapeutic as I navigate the waters of Wayne County government. What is the best way to start your day? That is your morning glory. When an ethically challenging situation arises, reflect back on your morning glory. Reflect back on your children. Reflect back on all the people who care about you. Reflect back on all the people who helped to shape and mold you. How disappointed would they be if there were an ethical breach? Keep a picture of your morning glory glued to your ethical bulletin board. With glory comes peace. Now that you have peace, you are in a position to spread that peace to others.

Remember I talked about how the individual morning glory flower lives only one day? I failed to mention something else: while the flowers die after a day, the plant survives. That's legacy. How you live each day will become your legacy. Like the flower, you may die but your teachings, and most importantly your example, live on.

EPILOGUE

Did You Win?

The trial lasted two weeks. The jury deliberated for one afternoon and went home for the evening. The following morning they returned at 8:30 a.m. sharp and resumed deliberations. In one hour they had a verdict. The client asked, "Is this a good sign?" He wanted to know if a quick verdict meant his resurrection or his demise. The client was told the quickness of the decision represented an all or nothing verdict. The jury either believed the government's theory or they did not. The client did not expect any compromises. The verdict would be either a home run or a strikeout.

The lawyer was impressed with the client's strength of character. The client had followed his personal code of ethics in the events that led to federal prosecution. He had advised co-workers on how to handle ethical dilemmas. At this moment, his advice was being weighed by the jury. The client never second-guessed his decision to reject a three-month guilty plea cap that was offered by the prosecution before charges were brought. Now, the client was facing a maximum of thirty years.

The case had taken its toll on the client. Emotionally he was drained. He had spent countless sleepless nights going over every piece of evidence in the case. Financially, the company where he worked was shut down due to the investigation. Now, he had no job. No matter what the outcome of the trial, he would be deeply worried about how he would be able to support his family. Physically, he lost a lot of weight. He actually looked like a different person. The strain and stress of the case looming over him for years had become an unbearable weight on his shoulders. But, he still stood strong on the ethical line he had drawn.

Once the jury took their seats the judge asked if they had reached a verdict. The foreperson said, "Yes." The judge instructed the foreperson to hand the verdict sheet to the court clerk. The judge instructed the court clerk to read the verdict. The court clerk read the case number, the name of the parties and the charges. This whole process, which took less than five minutes, seemed like an eternity. You could hear a pin drop in the courtroom. The client's wife and parents tightly held hands as they sat in the gallery.

With the picture of his family cupped in his hand, the client was looking for vindication. Vindication would lessen the emotional, financial and physical damage the case caused.

But at that moment he realized that vindication did not rest with the jury verdict. Vindication would be an internal thing.

The client now realized what was important in life. He would hug his wife tighter and spend more quality time with his parents. The verdict would have no influence in how he would love his boys unconditionally. He would teach his boys that a measure of a person is not what they have gained but what they had given. He would not pepper his sons with the question, "Did you win?" Instead he will ask, "Did you do the right thing?"

The pinnacle of his career would no longer be defined by how fast or high he climbed the corporate ladder. The pinnacle was using the gifts he was given to better others. Vindication was not dependent on title or position. A lit flame can ignite others and he was determined to be that spark. By spreading goodwill in all of his endeavors, he had found his calling. He found his morning glory. He was prepared to be a life-enhancer.

While the clerk of the court read the verdict, the client's face shone with an internal peace. He walked out of the courthouse into the bright sunshine with his head held high. He was ready to claim the ultimate victory and make "doing the right thing" his brand.